CD-ROM and Workbook
for Crisis Intervention

Rick A. Myer
Duquesne University

Richard Keith James
University of Memphis

BROOKS/COLE
CENGAGE Learning™

Australia • Brazil • Japan • Korea • Mexico • Singapore • Spain • United Kingdom • United States

Printed in the United States of America
  4 5 6 7 8 9 10 GP 11 10 09

ISBN-13: 978-0-495-22056-5
ISBN-10: 0-495-22056-6

For more information about our products,
contact us at:
academic.cengage.com

For permission to use material from this text or
product, submit a request online at
www.**cengage.com/permissions**
Any additional questions about permissions
can be submitted by email to
permissionrequest@cengage.com

Brooks/Cole, Cengage Learning
10 Davis Drive
Belmont, CA 94002-3098
USA

Asia
Thomson Learning
5 Shenton Way #01-01
UIC Building
Singapore 068808

Australia/New Zealand
Thomson Learning
102 Dodds Street
Southbank, Victoria 3006
Australia

Canada
Nelson
1120 Birchmount Road
Toronto, Ontario M1K 5G4
Canada

Europe/Middle East/South Africa
Thomson Learning
High Holborn House
50/51 Bedford Row
London WC1R 4LR
United Kingdom

Latin America
Thomson Learning
Seneca, 53
Colonia Polanco
11560 Mexico D.F.
Mexico

Spain/Portugal
Paraninfo
Calle/Magallanes, 25
28015 Madrid, Spain

PREFACE

Helping clients in crisis is different than counseling someone whom is seeking help through therapy. Although skills are similar to those used in traditional counseling, the application is very different. This book describes how to translate basic counseling skills for use in crisis situations. Throughout the book, examples are used to illustrate our ideas about crisis intervention. Our belief is that it is important to see the way the skills and strategies are applied. The CD-ROM that accompanies the book does just that. You will be able to see experts doing crisis intervention with three clients in crisis. These examples present the skills and strategies in action during each step of the intervention process.

Our primary objective is to introduce the material in a sequential, step-by-step manner. Each step builds on the previous one making it important to read the sections in order. Section One presents a model needed to understand the process of crisis intervention. This model is fluid and helps you to understand the intervention process rather than a rigid outline of the order for helping someone in crisis. Included in this section is what we call the "Rules of the Road". These rules are guidelines to help clinicians focus on the resolution of a crisis. Section Two introduces you to nine crisis intervention strategies and three levels of treatment. The section describes each strategy and provides rationale for the levels of treatment. The case of Mary, introduced in this section, is used to demonstrate the application of the strategies as well as the levels of treatment. Section Three integrates the material in the first two sections. The case of Mary is used again to illustrate this process. Learning activities and exercises for this section in included in the CD-ROM. Section Four continues the integration of the first three sections of the book. Verbatims from two case examples are used to demonstrate the process of crisis intervention. The crisis workers in these situations use different intervention styles to help the clients move toward resolution of the crisis. Case one is a severe reaction to a crisis involving a mother whose son was injured while on a school field trip. This case illustrates a crisis in which the crisis worker must calm a hysterical client. Case two examines a crisis that is complicated by substance abuse. In this case, the client is a recovering addict who is divorced and recently lost his job. As a result, his former wife will not allow him to visit their children. These cases will appear on the CD-ROM along with transcripts in the workbook. Accompanying this section will be exercises to assist students in learning crisis intervention strategies.

ACKNOWLEDGMENTS

Communicating the fundamental nature of crisis intervention proved to be an interesting task, being both simple and complex. The basic strategies in crisis intervention appear straightforward and easy to identify. However, the complexity becomes apparent when applying these strategies to the diversity of crises that can be experienced. Our hope is that this workbook is useful in developing and refining your approach for crisis intervention. Use the examples as starting points to create your own style of helping people resolve crises.

We want to express our appreciation to the many people involved in helping us complete this project. Comments from the reviewers of early drafts alerted us about the need to stay focused and be clear about the meaning of a crisis. The patience and humor of the production professionals was needed as we struggled through the process of taping the video segments. The editors and staff of Wadsworth were equally patient and helpful as we worked with them to develop the CD-ROM. We also appreciated the School of Education, Duquesne University's willingness to use its facilities for taping the video segments.

We also extend our appreciation to the University of Memphis Crisis Research Team of the Department of Counseling, Educational Psychology, and Research for their assistance in developing the case scenarios. Catherine Addy's assistance and willingness to participate as a client in a scenario was invaluable. The Crisis Research Group of the Department of Counseling, Psychology, and Special Education, Duquesne University also helped as we video taped the segments. Special thanks to Tina Bigante, Ed Cadwallader, Jay Darr, Holly Moore, Leslie Slagel, Scott Tracy, and Mimi Yablonsky who assisted us in preparing and taping the video segments. Their assistance was extremely valuable in the completion of the video segments.

Finally, we thank our families and their patience as we developed and completed the project. Thanks Susan and Sarah for the support.

TABLE OF CONTENTS

FIGURES

TABLES

SECTION ONE

Introduction

Most probably crisis intervention was introduced as a form of counseling as far back as the first attempted exorcism of cavemen's "demons" by ice age medicine men. However, in the last 30 years interest crisis intervention has skyrocketed resulting in it growing into a field of its own. The growth of the community mental health movement and advent of crisis hotlines (Kleespies & Blackburn, 1998; Seely, 1997) along with ongoing concern regarding suicide (Rudd et al., 1999; Sanchez, 2001) have combined to support the growth of crisis intervention. Recent dramatic events such as the September 11th terrorist attacks on the World Trade Centers and Pentagon, Columbine School shootings, Washington DC sniper attacks along with numerous other less shocking disasters and crises have also provoked awareness for the need for the competent delivery of crisis intervention services. Others issues that have contributed to the expansion of crisis intervention include the continued problem of interpersonal violence (Eisler, 1995; Kreidler & England, 1990; Salter, 1988; Walker, 1989) and the belief that treatment immediately following being victimized by others or experiencing a disaster can prevent long-term mental health problems (Raphael & Wilson, 2000;Ursano, Grieger, & McCarroll, 1996). Changes in the delivery of services for mental health caused by managed care have also been identified as a source for the extension of crisis intervention (Kolski, Avriette, & Jongsma, 2001). Together these issues along with others have combined to establish crisis intervention as a subspecialty in the field of mental health.

If your first introduction to crisis intervention is through the use of the CD-ROM that accompanies this manual, we believe there are some basic components about the field of crisis intervention you ought to be familiar with to guide your learning. To that end, we are going to provide you with a brief overview of the field and then give you some basic rules of the road that will help you as you grapple with the scenarios on the CD-ROM and become skillful in using crisis intervention techniques. Finally, we will give you a demonstration case in this section that will give you an idea of how we go about the business.

What Is A Crisis?

There are many definitions of what constitutes a crisis sufficient to bring a person to therapy (Belkin, 1984; Brammer, 1985; Caplan, 1961, 1964; Carkhuff & Berenson, 1977). We define crisis as: *the perception of an event or situation as an intolerable difficulty that exceeds the resources and coping mechanisms of the person, and unless the person gains relief the crisis has the potential to cause severe affective, cognitive, and behavioral malfunctioning. Crisis is both universal and idiosyncratic. No matter how tough or resilient, given the right constellation of circumstances, no one is immune from breakdown. Crisis is also idiosyncratic because what one person may successfully overcome another may not, even though the circumstances are virtually the same* (James & Gilliland, 2001, p. 3-5).

Figure 1.1 Overlap Model

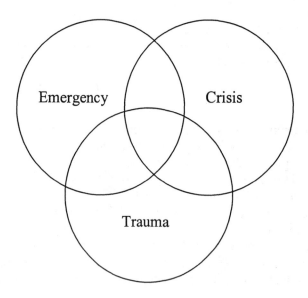

In the past 10 years debate has surfaced regarding the need to differentiate between psychological emergencies and psychological crises (Callahan, 1994). Although the concepts have common characteristics, close examination shows differences can be identified. Adding to the confusion is the concept of trauma, a term also used synonymously with crisis. Again, overlap exists between the concepts, but also differences. Figure 1.1 shows the relationships among these terms. Note that for each concept, some characteristics are unique whereas others overlap. The overlap can be between two of the concepts or may be common to all three. Sorting through these similarities and differences is important in order to provide the appropriate level and type of intervention (Callahan, 1994).

Emergency

A characteristic of psychological emergencies is that people are unable to function in a normal manner and can be described as being incompetent, unable to assume personal responsibility (Baldwin, 1978). Callahan (1998) adds these people are defenseless, and because their judgment is impaired they are incapable of caring for themselves or others. Permanent damage, psychological or physical, is always a possibility for people experiencing a psychological emergency. Many times these individuals have either threatened or attempted suicide or homicide. At other times, people in crisis place themselves or others in danger because of neglect in not using common sense safety measures or precautions. A person who, because of using drugs loses consciousness leaving several very young children to care for themselves, is an example. Another example, is a person who has a psychotic episode and walks down the middle of a busy highway not comprehending the danger. Although these people are not intentionally suicidal or homicidal, they are incompetent to care for themselves or others. An imminent risk of permanent harm is present.

Another characteristic of psychological emergencies is the suddenness or abruptness with which it appears (Callahan, 1998). A friend overdoses on drugs or attempts suicide, a family member experiences a psychotic episode or undergoes a significant personality change and enters a dissociative state. Problems such as these are dramatic and generally involve imminent risk of psychological or physical harm. Something needs to be done as quickly as possible to prevent possible irreversible physical or psychological damage to self and others. Although these problems seem to materialize out of nowhere, more often than not these emergencies developed over an extended time period (Callahan, 1998). As we stated earlier, in a perfect world people would address difficulties and resolve problems to prevent them from reaching the level of being an emergency. Once at this level, interventions must be decisive and immediate. Hospitalization, voluntary or involuntary, is frequently needed to achieve the safety of individuals. The principal goal is to protect individuals from harming themselves and others.

Crisis

The defining characteristic of people in crisis is being overwhelmed and experiencing a sense of disequilibrium. Their typical ways of coping with problems are ineffective or may be insufficient to resolve the problem. Similar to people having a psychological emergency, people in crisis may be vulnerable to varying degrees. However, the vulnerability does not place them in immediate danger of harming themselves or others. For example, a woman who was just diagnosed with breast cancer or a man who discovers his teenage daughter is pregnant may be in crisis, but the level of vulnerability or threat of harm is usually not elevated to the point of needing hospitalization. Yet, the chance to develop long-term emotional, behavioral, and cognitive problems exists unless people avail themselves of help either from professionals, paraprofessionals, or other support people such as family and friends. More often than not when people get support from others long-term problems do not develop.

Crises are classified into four types: (a) developmental; (b) situational; (c) existential; and (d) systemic (James & Gilliland, 2001). These types are determined by the precipitating event or events for the crisis. Although at times the characteristics are similar or overlap, each are distinct enough to necessitate separate descriptions.

Developmental crises occur when events in the normal flux and flow of human growth are disrupted by a dramatic shift that precipitates an abnormal response. Graduation from college, marriage, a first child, job change, or retirement are all key developmental benchmarks that call for dramatic shifts in how a person operates and may occasion a crisis event (Brammer, 1985).

Situational crises occur when an uncommon event occurs that the individual has no way of forecasting or controlling. Automobile accidents, rapes, shootings, sudden illnesses and death, job loss, and divorce are all examples of unforeseen, shocking, sudden, and intense traumatic events that are far out of the realm of normal functioning (Brammer, 1985).

Existential crises are those inner conflicts that accompany important human issues of joy, happiness, love, responsibility, goal-orientation, and self-concept. Existential crisis occur when individuals suddenly realize that some important intrapersonal aspect of their lives will never be fulfilled. Finding out that a major league baseball career is beyond one's skills after a great collegiate career, after thirty years realizing that an ill conceived marriage is doomed, never taking a risk or an adventure before being bedridden with arthritis, and a death bed review of one's life as meaningless are examples of crises of self-purpose and self-worth (Brammer, 1985).

Systemic crises are different from the previous types in that these crises ripple out into large segments of the population and the environment itself (James & Gilliland, 2001). Natural disasters such as hurricanes wreak havoc on all parts of the ecological system. Besides death and injury, basic human necessities such as food and shelter are lost. Infrastructure services are destroyed and the means of employment are lost because the businesses where people worked are no longer in existence. Man-made disasters such as 9-11, the Oklahoma City Federal Building bombing and the Columbine school massacre strike not only the immediate victims but through extensive media exposure, psychologically impact and traumatize people throughout the world. As a result, the kinds of psychological intervention applied to these crisis domains tends to be very different than the normal course of psychotherapy.

Another characteristic of people in crisis is that they generally reestablish a sense of equilibrium in about six weeks (Callahan, 1998). During this time, intervention should focus on helping the client return to a pre-crisis level of functioning, be realistic (Cournoyer, 1996), and focus on the reactions to the crisis, not attempt to help people make major life or personality changes. However, many people experience problems because of the crisis after they have regained a sense of equilibrium. These problems can be triggered by anniversary dates or holidays. The first Christmas or wedding anniversary after the death of a significant person are examples. At these times, people's reactions may be similar to the reactions they experienced at the time of the crisis but usually not at the same intensity.

Trauma

Traumas occur when normal patterns of development are altered due to people perceiving an enormous sense of helplessness and threat (van der Kolk & McFarlane, 1996). According to van der Kolk and McFarlane, in this situation, memory of the trauma is not integrated; instead, it develops an existence of its own independent of previous schema. People's beliefs about the world are permanently changed. A single incident such as witnessing a murder, exposure to natural disasters like a tornado, a family member or close friend being killed in an automobile accident, and so on can result in people being traumatized. People also experience psychological trauma due to episodic events that occur over extended periods of time (Pynoos, Steinberg, & Goejian, 1996). An obvious example is children who witness or are a victim of prolonged domestic violence. The normal development of these children can be interrupted and disrupted to the point they are not able to form healthy relationships.

Another characteristic of trauma is the extended fixation on the event causing the problems. The adage that time heals all wounds does not apply for people who are traumatized. The trauma continues to intrude into people's lives well beyond the typical six week period of a person who is experiencing a crisis (McFarlane & Yehuda, 1996). The intrusions can take many shapes. Nightmares and flashbacks are not unusual. Intense emotions such as rage and panic can also be felt by people who are traumatized. Some people reenact the trauma time and time again. The trauma remains rooted in peoples' lives so that it remains a contemporary experience, not being something accepted as belonging to the past (van der Kolk & McFarlane, 1996).

What Is Crisis Intervention?

It is important to understand that much counseling starts as crisis intervention. In a perfect world, people would be aware of problems and issues they face and would be proactive in taking care of them before these erupted into crisis proportions. Clearly though, we live in a far less than perfect world and as a result, most counseling starts in a reactive mode because the individual has not been willing to address difficult choices. In fact, by not making a choice, the individual makes a choice to do nothing. Doing nothing invariably means the problem will get worse, and if enough time is spent doing nothing, a crisis will inevitably erupt.

Yet, not all crisis counseling results from an individual's failure to tackle a problem head-on. Again in a perfect world, there would be no crime, no natural or man-made disasters, no sexual assault, no sudden traumatic physical injuries or death, no financial ruin, no war, no family violence, and no negative psychological impact from any of these events. In a not-so-perfect world we are all subject to experience such events and may have little choice in the matter. The traumatic wake of those events can breed crises of immense proportions for individuals. If not dealt with, these events can transition from immediate overwhelming distress from the crisis event into Acute Stress Disorder and finally to Post Traumatic Stress Disorder itself.

Crisis intervention targets the affective, behavioral, and cognitive distortions generated by neglecting problems or unexpected traumatic events and helps people recognize and correct their feelings, behaviors, and perceptions to approximate more normal pre-crisis functioning. Treatment, therefore, focuses on a single issue (Cournoyer, 1996) that is of immediate concern with the purpose being to help people reclaim a sense of equilibrium. Although other problematic issues may be present and/or identified, these should be discussed at the conclusion of the crisis intervention process. Take for example a woman seeking assistance from a domestic violence shelter. Although the woman may also have experienced abuse as a child, crisis intervention must concentrate on addressing the issue related to the domestic violence. Engaging in psychological archeological digs to unearth and resolve the issues related to the child abuse is not appropriate, and possibly unethical. Granted the abuse may have a relationship to the domestic violence, yet only after the woman has regained a sense of equilibrium should the child abuse be addressed. And then posing the need to deal with the child abuse as a recommendation is the most ethical course of action.

Focusing quickly on the problem is also important in crisis intervention (Kleespies, Deleppo, Mori, & Niles, 1998). Spending too much time developing rapport generally results in people thinking their crisis is being ignored. The traditional first interview approach of allowing the therapeutic relationship to unfold and gathering a wide range of psychosocial information simply does not work. Instead, an action-oriented approach that rapidly engages clients is essential. As rapidly and briefly as possible information relevant to the crisis should be gathered. Information regarding clients' feelings about the crisis, behaviors they have or are using to resolve the crisis, and perceptions about the meaning of the crisis is the information that is needed. The information should be directly applicable to helping clients resolve the crisis and reestablish their pre-crisis level of functioning (Myer, 2001).

Flexibility in scheduling is also needed in crisis intervention. The typical 50-minute hour may not work for people in crisis. Sessions for crisis intervention take as long as they take. Sometimes this means that a crisis intervention session may last hours, whereas at other times only 10 minutes is needed. Some clients need multiple sessions over several weeks that use varying amounts of time for each session. Some sessions may be 15 minutes whereas others may resemble the traditional 50-minute hour. Other clients may need only one session that lasts a short amount of time. The telephone is an important tool to create flexibility in scheduling. Asking clients to contact you or you contacting them by telephone allows more contacts for shorter periods of time. The guideline is you work with clients as long as needed especially with clients who are potentially dangerous to self or others.

Crisis Counseling Skills

To deal with emergencies and crises, and to a lesser degree traumas, calls for a variety of skills from the worker that do not fit neatly into what might be expected of a more traditional therapist. The ability to use accurate listening and responding skills, assess, analyze, synthesize, diagnose, explore alternatives and plan and solve problems are all as important in crisis intervention as they would be in traditional therapy. The skills most often used in crisis intervention are listed in Appendix A. These skills are all that is needed to be effective. However, the crisis worker will typically have little time, support, or resources to do these activities. Crisis intervention is a stand-up act where time frames are exceedingly short and rapid decisions have to be made. Because of rapidly changing conditions and the volatile atmosphere that surrounds a crisis, the worker will have to be exceedingly adaptive. Crisis work also requires a great deal of emotional energy, poise and calmness in emergency conditions, quick mental reflexes, and creativity in approaching complex and seemingly insolvable problems or insurmountable conditions. Day-in-and-day-out, crisis work is clearly not for everyone because of the demands it places upon the individual. In that regard, the burnout rate for crisis workers is exceedingly high (Distler, 1990; Freudenberger, 1974; Maslach, 1982; McRaith, 1991).

What then is expected of a crisis worker in dealing with a client in crisis? Unlike traditional, long-term therapy, the creation of a cure or the movement of a client to more self-actualized behavior is not an end-goal. The immediate and overriding objective of the crisis worker is to contain the situation, stabilize the client, stop the escalation of emotional disequilibrium and disorganization and, hopefully, return the client to as close to pre-crisis functioning as possible. At that point in time the crisis worker's job is done and the client may be referred, if needed, to long term therapy where systemic change and increased functioning is the goal. The focus of the scenarios you will encounter in the CD are targeted directly on the foregoing ideas. The following model depicts how we go about doing that.

The Six-Step Model of Crisis Intervention

Our own model for crisis intervention is based on the Six-Step Crisis Intervention model (see Figure 1.2) developed by Gilliland and James (1989). The steps do not necessarily function as discrete entities. Rather, at times, some of the steps may be transposed or they may be integrated as a smoothly flowing process. Overarching the six steps is a constant and dynamic assessment of evaluating the client's past and present situational crisis in regard to his or her: ability to cope, response to personal threat, amount of lethality, degree of mobility and type and amount of direct action needed by the crisis worker. The six-step model may be loosely divided into two major categories of *listening* and *acting*. In the first three steps, the emphasis of the crisis worker will be on listening by: attending, observing, understanding, empathizing, accepting, and being nonjudgmental, caring, respectful, and genuine. In the second three steps, the emphasis of the crisis worker will be on acting by: becoming involved in the intervention at a nondirective, collaborative, or directive level according to the assessed needs of the client and the availability of environmental supports and coping mechanisms. Given our qualifiers about how the model is put into operation, listed below are the six steps with some helpful "rules of the road" for putting them into operation.

Figure 1.2 Systematic Model

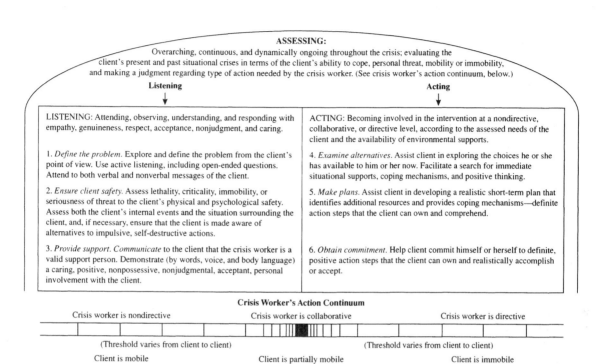

ASSESSING:
Overarching, continuous, and dynamically ongoing throughout the crisis; evaluating the client's present and past situational crises in terms of the client's ability to cope, personal threat, mobility or immobility, and making a judgment regarding type of action needed by the crisis worker. (See crisis worker's action continuum, below.)

Listening → / Acting ↓

LISTENING: Attending, observing, understanding, and responding with empathy, genuineness, respect, acceptance, nonjudgment, and caring.	ACTING: Becoming involved in the intervention at a nondirective, collaborative, or directive level, according to the assessed needs of the client and the availability of environmental supports.
1. *Define the problem.* Explore and define the problem from the client's point of view. Use active listening, including open-ended questions. Attend to both verbal and nonverbal messages of the client.	4. *Examine alternatives.* Assist client in exploring the choices he or she has available to him or her now. Facilitate a search for immediate situational supports, coping mechanisms, and positive thinking.
2. *Ensure client safety.* Assess lethality, criticality, immobility, or seriousness of threat to the client's physical and psychological safety. Assess both the client's internal events and the situation surrounding the client, and, if necessary, ensure that the client is made aware of alternatives to impulsive, self-destructive actions.	5. *Make plans.* Assist client in developing a realistic short-term plan that identifies additional resources and provides coping mechanisms—definite action steps that the client can own and comprehend.
3. *Provide support.* Communicate to the client that the crisis worker is a valid support person. Demonstrate (by words, voice, and body language) a caring, positive, nonpossessive, nonjudgmental, acceptant, personal involvement with the client.	6. *Obtain commitment.* Help client commit himself or herself to definite, positive action steps that the client can own and realistically accomplish or accept.

Crisis Worker's Action Continuum

Crisis worker is nondirective	Crisis worker is collaborative	Crisis worker is directive
(Threshold varies from client to client)		(Threshold varies from client to client)
Client is mobile	Client is partially mobile	Client is immobile

The crisis worker's level of action/involvement may be anywhere on the continuum according to a valid and realistic assessment of the client's level of mobility/immobility.

We have added *Rules of the Road* to the Six-Step Model. These are guidelines that help crisis workers as they think about and put together responses for clients. The guidelines are practical suggestions that generally correspond to a specific Step in the model. However, since the model is fluid rather that static, Rules of the Road from one Step may be applied to and used in another Step in the model. This situation is particularly evident as you transition from one step to another. For example, as you move from Step One to Step Two, the *Rules of the Road* from Step One may still be appropriate and applied in Step Two.

Step 1. Defining the Problem

While time limits may severely compress the crisis worker's ability to define the problem, nevertheless, it is critical that the worker attempt to gain as clear an understanding as possible about what is going on with the client at this point in time. Care must be taken not to confuse an event with the crisis. Take for example, a father whose 15-year-old daughter just announced that she is pregnant. The father is active in church, owns a business, and volunteers in the community. At first glance the crisis may seem to be the pregnancy, but it could also be the father may be embarrassed at his church. He might also be concerned about a decrease in business if his customers discovered his daughter was pregnant or fear of losing his standing in the community. Therefore, it is also important to understand the meaning given to the event by the client. How and what has changed to now put the client in a crisis state are questions to be answered. Further, how are the client's affect, behavior, and cognition now different than before the crisis occurred?

7

Table 1.1 Rules of the Road

RULES OF THE ROAD

Step 1. Defining the Problem	1. Communicate caring attitude 2. Establish contact 3. Explore meaning of crisis
Step 2. Ensuring Safety	1. Use directive, closed end questions 2. Determining degree of lethality 3. Take immediate action to ensure safety of oneself, the client, or significant others. 4. Reinforce the client's proactive, safe behavior. 5. Make owning statements about your responsibility. 6. Use the Triage Severity Scale as a basis of making decision on client disposition.
Step 3. Providing Support	1. Make very clear owning statements that the client really does count for something. 2. Positively reinforce even the most minimal client movement. 3. Searching for external supports is critical in providing continuing help to get through the crisis.
Step 4. Examining Alternatives	1. Use situational support mechanisms. 2. Use previously successful coping mechanisms. 3. Use environmental resources. 4. Generate positive and constructive thinking patterns. 5. Reinforcing taking action.
Step 5. Making Plans	1. Emphasize short-term goals. 2. Make concrete plans.
Step 6. Obtaining Commitment	1. Review plan. 2. Establish Responsibility.

Defining the Problem-Rules of the Road

1. <u>Communicate Caring Attitude.</u> The core crisis worker facilitative qualities of empathy, genuineness, acceptance, concreteness, and unconditional positive regard (Cormier & Cormier, 1991) are especially important for clients who may have few qualities in the present moment that would endear them to the crisis worker. As badly as clients in crisis may be acting, they are attempting to problem solve to the best of their abilities.

   CW: (Dealing with a client who is just coming off drugs brought into an inpatient facility by the police in restraints who looks, smells, feels, and acts bad).

   CL: Nobody gives a shit about me (vomits with dry heaves, shaking) Why should you two-bit do-gooder SOB? I'd as just soon be dead but the friggin' cops brought me in here. Now buzz off and leave me alone you jerk. Can't you see how I look and feel you clueless idiot. You don't know nuthin' about the troubles I've seen (Looks menacingly at worker).

   CW: No I don't know anything about the troubles you've seen, Jake, but I do know that you voluntarily got into the police car without jumping off the bridge. That means there is some part of you that cares about living and while I don't much like the way you're acting right now, I want very much to find that part of you that does want to live and get out of the drug scene and all that goes with it.

2. <u>Establish Contact.</u> Establishing contact with clients who are in crisis is not like the development of rapport in individual counseling (Kleespies, Deleppo, Mori, & Niles, 1998). Crisis workers should assume the role of the helper and confidently communicate that to clients. An important variable in establishing contact is the severity of clients' reactions. The more severe the reaction, the more crisis workers should assume contact has been established.

   CL: Who did you say you are anyway? And why the hell are you talking to me? No one can help me now. Just leave me alone.

   CW: I am talking to you because I can help and I won't leave you alone. It may seem hopeless right now, but I have helped people worse off than you. Yea, there are people worse off than you. Like I said, I can help you find a part of you that knows life can be better.

3. <u>Explore Meaning of Crisis.</u> A critical aspect of crisis intervention is defining the crisis from the client's perspective (Callahan, 1998; James & Gilliland, 2001). You must work to understand the problem as clients see it.

   CW: Tell me, what happened to make you want to jump off the bridge today?

   CL: Man I don't know. My fucking life isn't worth living. Besides my girl friend just kicked me out of the house.

   CW: That does sound bad. I get the idea she is important to you.

   CL: You got that right. I need her.

   CW: I hear that. Sounds like you don't want to be alone.

9

Step 2. <u>Safety</u>

Because of the high potential for violence to oneself or to others in a crisis situation, safety is an important key step. It is absolutely paramount that crisis workers be aware of safety considerations for their clients, others, and most importantly, for themselves. This step cuts across all of the other steps of crisis intervention. Thus, safety needs are constantly assessed from start to finish. The Triage Assessment Scale (TAF) (Myer, Williams, Ottens, & Schmidt, 1992) located in Appendix B, is an excellent visual and verbal assessment device for determining the seriousness of a client's safety needs. The TAF assesses the client's affective responses on dimensions of anger/hostility, fear/anxiety, and sadness/melancholy; cognitive responses on dimensions of loss, threat, and transgression; and behavioral dimensions that assess if the client is immobile, actively engaging in or attempting to avoid the crisis. The TAF rates clients numerically on affective, behavioral, and cognitive dimensions of functioning by comparing written scale definitions against what the crisis worker observes and hears the client doing and saying. Each of the three scales has a 1 to 10 range for a total possible score of 30. Low scale scores that range from 3 to 14 indicate minimum impairment, scale scores from 15 to 23 indicate moderate impairment, and scores from 24 to 30 indicate severe impairment. The higher end scores are indicative that the client needs to be placed in a setting where he or she will be secure and safe. A score on a single scale of 10 also indicates the client should be placed in a setting that can protect him or her. Suffice it to say that few clients who are in crisis will be in the low impairment range while many may be angrily acting out against others or attempting to do harm to themselves.

Safety Needs-Rules of the Road

1. <u>Be Direct</u>. In considering safety needs, the crisis worker cannot be bashful about using directive questions to determine client lethality towards self and others. Whereas closed-end questions are often seen as inappropriate in a standard counseling regimen, in crisis counseling they are often times highly effective in determining safety needs. Straight forwardly asking a client, "Are you planning on killing yourself?" demands a "Yes!" or "No!" response from the client. Rather than driving the client to consider such action as a beginning crisis worker might fear, such directive questions actually give the client permission to start talking about lethality issues and gain the crisis worker credibility as someone sensitive enough to perceive that the client is indeed having such terrible thoughts.

> *CL:* I dunno, sometimes it seems such a hassle, not worth trying to go on.

> *CW:* Jake, is what you're saying is that you're planning on ending your life?

2. <u>Determining degree of lethality</u>. Although indicators are used, there is no precise formula for determining degree of lethality. However, the more clear and concrete the method, motive, opportunity, and means the more lethal the client becomes.

> *CW:* So if you were to kill yourself how would you do it?

> *CL:* Easy! I'd wait until everybody left for work at my folk's house. I could get in the garage door. The old man's antique Ford pick-up is in there. I know where the key is. I'd turn it on and that would be it. Poetic justice, me dead in the old man's pride and joy. I sure never was.

> *CW:* When would that be?

CL: I dunno! Soon, next week maybe.

3. <u>Take immediate action to ensure safety of oneself, the client , or significant others</u>. Depending upon the degree of lethality manifested by the client, the crisis worker needs to have specific action counseling tools available such as anti-suicide contracts, places of safety, and so forth. The crisis worker also needs to have all the information needed (e.g., phone numbers, hours, location) for immediate referral sources such as hospitals, law enforcement, and emergency personnel that may be contacted.

> *CW:* What you just said tells me that you are deadly serious about this. I do not want to see that happen and I don't think your girlfriend does. What I want to do is to get her in here and let's get you some breathing space from this awful sense of dread, foreboding, and hopelessness you feel. If you can't agree to that I need to make a 911 call and get you to a safe place.

4. <u>Reinforce the client's proactive, safe behavior.</u> Any approximate towards safe behavior and away from lethal behavior should be reinforced immediately even though the client might not be completely adaptive.

> *CW:* I think the very fact that you're here says you really want to work this out, and that is an excellent first step.

5. <u>Make owning statements about your responsibility.</u> The client should be very clear that you will respond to any crisis of potential lethality in a proactive, immediate manner.

> *CW:* As long as you are under my care I will not let you hurt yourself and I want to be very clear that I will do everything to keep that from happening.

6. <u>Use the triage scale as a basis of making decisions on client disposition.</u> The TAF has good reliability (Watters, 1997) and is rapidly learned by beginners in crisis intervention. It has been taught in one session to nurses, police officers, social workers, psychologists, licensed professional counselors, school counselors and undergraduate students who had little familiarity with crisis work. The TAF provides a baseline to make decisions about what needs to happen to the client and how directive you need to be.

Step 3. <u>Providing Support.</u>

Unlike a standard therapeutic regimen where the crisis worker may be wary of being too directive in providing emotional or other kinds of support for fear of breeding client dependency, in crisis intervention, therapists must communicate to clients that they are prized, accepted, and valued.

Supportive Needs - Rules of the Road

1. <u>Make very clear owning statements that the client really does count for something.</u> Typically, clients in crisis have received numerous messages from others in their past that they aren't worth much. It is reasonable to expect that by the time the client reaches this point, his or her self-esteem and self-concept will be very low.

> *CW:* You may feel like your parents, your friends, and everybody else may not believe in you right now, but you do count for something. The very fact that you came down off that bridge and the fact that you are talking to me right now says you want to be alive and that counts for a lot. I'm glad you made that choice.

2. The crisis worker positively reinforces even the most minimal client movement. Much like reinforcing non-lethal behavior, any adaptive, normative behavior is immediately reinforced. The fact that the client was able to get to a clinic after a severe psychotic break, call a spouse abuse line after a beating, or follow crisis worker instructions to take one deep breath when for the five minutes beforehand the client was racked by sobbing are behavioral specific events that the crisis worker can reinforce. Even a little judicious use of humor may be used as a tension reduction mechanism.

> *CW:* (Chuckling) Well, I think we are making progress. At least in that last exchange you didn't say terrible things about my mother or use any other four letter Anglo-Saxon colloquialisms in regard to my body parts. Notice how you are much calmer now. Your hands are just barely trembling. I believe if you took just one more deep breath and let it out slowly, that's it, just feel the warm air going out your airway and feel the load lift off your chest a bit. I believe we can get out of the middle of the street and sit down on that bench over there out of this heat and relax a little.

3. Searching for external social supports is critical in providing continuing help to get through the crisis. This rule is important from the standpoint that clients may be at a point in their lives when they believe they have no personal social support at all. Due to a variety of negative emotions and self-attributions clients may believe that no one cares about them when in fact that is not the case. A primary job of the crisis worker is attempting to find new support persons or help the client reestablish contact with previous support systems. Clients may typically dismiss many such support persons because they have aggrieved them in some way in the past, but if the crisis worker is diligent and persistent, even the most socially isolated clients will most probably have some support person to provide short term aid to them.

> *CW:* You did say you had a girlfriend. And that she was really distraught when you left to go out tonight. How can I get in touch with her?

If the crisis worker cannot find any other support person, then the worker must temporarily assume that role.

> *CW:* I will ride in the police car with you to the hospital. I won't let the cops hurt you. I'll also stay with you at the hospital until you get checked in and settled. I'll check back at the hospital this afternoon to see if your social worker has contacted you.

Step 4. Examining Alternatives

Clients in crisis often believe they have no options left, that the crisis has left them so immobilized that they can't retake control of their lives. Examining alternatives may be thought of in a variety of ways and includes searching for situational supports, generating coping mechanisms, and engaging in positive thinking. While crisis counseling is highly focused on the here-and-now and a real time orientation, attempting to find behaviors and environmental resources that have helped in the past and that the client may have forgotten or dismissed as ineffective is important to restoring control by starting to generate alternatives to the present dilemma. Two critical components that are often missing in the lives of crisis clients are social involvement and positive addicting behaviors. Alfred Adler (1958) and William Glasser (1976), two noted psychotherapists and personality theorists have spent a great deal of time writing about these concepts. To get out of the psychological quagmire that crisis clients often find themselves in, it is necessary to become re-involved with other people socially and to reestablish activities that are fulfilling and growth promoting.

Examining Alternatives-Rules of the Road

1. <u>Use situational support mechanisms.</u> Situational support mechanisms are people, places, and things known to the client from his or her present or past which are helpful in providing the client with psychological anchors and keeping them in homeostasis. Because of change in geographic location, personal friends leaving or dying, economic downturns, or any other of a number of life changes, clients may be unable to perceive that they have situational supports available to them, and are embarrassed or afraid to seek out new supports.

> *CL:* I came to Maine for the job, nothing else. Moved 1200 miles from home and don't know a soul here besides the people I work with. I must have been nuts. I am so lonely I think I am going to lose my mind. No wonder I feel like going back on drugs.
>
> *CW:* Besides work and your family back in Illinois, where did you spend time?
>
> *CL:* At the local parish church, playing basketball and softball on the Knights of Columbus team. I had a good time with those guys.
>
> *CW:* Is there not a Catholic church here in Bangor?
>
> *CL:* Yeah, but I don't really know anybody, not like home. I went once. I don't even think they play softball up here unless they do it with snowshoes.
>
> *CW:* But you could go check that out and find out. Actually talk to the priest.

2. <u>Use previously successful coping mechanisms.</u> Coping mechanisms that have been previously successful are often forgotten or dismissed and discounted by clients in crisis. Behaviors and environmental resources that the client might use to get through the present crisis are also not accessed because client's have either forgotten or are unaware these resources are available. While clients may protest that those mechanisms are unavailable or unattainable in their present situation, the crisis workers may have resources available to help the client put those coping behaviors in place. Coping behaviors may range from personal stress reduction such as knitting, cleaning house, playing the piano, jogging and fishing to interactive social activities such as delivering meals on wheels, helping build houses for habitat for humanity, dancing, and playing cards.

> *CL:* You won't believe this, but I was into playing the tuba. I was in a brass band in Illinois. Real relaxing. I sorta got away from that after I got into doing coke. Hocked the tuba.
>
> *CW:* I may be able to put you in contact with a professor at the university. They have this community tuba band, I've seen them play at different places. They're all ages, shapes and sizes.

While crisis workers don't necessarily have to know about how to access a brass band, they do need to query their clients about pastimes that are often forgotten, neglected, or dismissed as being inconsequential.

3. <u>Use environmental resources.</u> Environmental resources may be considered from two perspectives, the client's and the crisis worker's. Generating environmental resources may involve finding out if the client belongs to a support group, a service organization, a church, or fraternal organization and calling on those organizations for assistance. Many times clients will feel that like significant others in

their past, they have alienated these organizations or they are no longer available because of being in a different geographic locale.

The crisis worker's own list of environmental resources such as state social services, insurance, social security and pension benefits, EAP programs, and charitable organizations may be important if the client is suffering severe financial burdens from the crisis. Crisis workers need to have extensive knowledge of environmental resources and referral sources for clients and be able to access them quickly.

> *CW:* Let's just look up on the local website Community LINC and see what there are in the way of softball teams that play with or without snowshoes. Even if it isn't church related, my guess is that you might find some friends.

4. <u>Generate positive and constructive thinking patterns</u>. Positive and constructive thinking patterns are critical in getting clients out of negative irrational thinking which tends to dominate a crisis client's cognitive processes. Because the client's mind may be spinning out-of-control from the onslaught of the crisis, it may be very difficult to keep the client's thinking linear and positive. Changing negative self-talk and nay-saying to positive injunctions is important in getting a client to start believing that there are ways out of the crisis.

> *CW:* You say you can't play ball anymore; that it would be too embarrassing. You are out of practice both as a softball player and a tuba player. But you don't know how good the others are, and I've got to think that playing on snowshoes levels the playing field. So can you say to yourself, "Jake on snowshoes might be interesting to see running to first base or playing the tuba?"

5. <u>Reinforcing taking action.</u> Many times, crisis clients are so self-involved with what is happening to them, they have difficulty hearing what is being said or requested of them. Oftentimes the crisis worker will have to use very directive declarative statements and use what the Canter's (Canter & Canter, 1982) call the broken record routine of keeping a client on track with the crisis worker. Therefore, it is not uncommon for the therapist to have to repeat over and over what they may be requesting the client to do and to ask for acknowledgement that the client indeed heard the crisis worker.

> *CL:* I don't know, I just get so down all the time. What's the use?

> *CW:* We are talking about softball and tubas, not being down. Now how are we going to check these out?

Step 5-<u>Making Plans</u>

Most therapeutic endeavors make action plans with their clients to carry out what has been learned in therapy into their everyday lives. Crisis intervention is no different and considers planning a major component of returning the client to a state of pre-crisis equilibrium. What is different about crisis intervention is that planning is compressed in time. As opposed to weekly, monthly, or even lifetime plans in a traditional therapeutic regimen, crisis intervention views planning in terms of minutes, hours, and days.

The locus of planning in a traditional therapeutic setting would mainly be from the client with minimal crisis worker direction. In crisis intervention the crisis worker will usually assume a highly collaborative role and will at times be very directive in helping the client get through the next few minutes, hours, or days. In crisis intervention, the crisis worker will often be highly involved in planning as to who and what supportive persons and services will be needed and how and what coping mechanisms will be put in place because the client may not have the mental and physical resources to do so without considerable help. The agitated drug addict coming off crack, the violent PTSD client who has had a severe flashback, the stunned rape victim brought to a trauma center, and the shocked survivor whose family has just been wiped out in a car accident are typical examples of clients who have little personal resources at the moment to formulate their own plans of action.

However, as much as possible, crisis intervention attempts to create and return enough control and autonomy so that plans can be owned by clients and they don't become dependent on either support persons or the crisis worker.

Making Plans – Rules of the Road

1. <u>Emphasize short-term goals</u>. Some clients experiencing a crisis want to make decisions that have long-term implications. A person who is addicted to drugs may decide to open a half-way house for others having the same problem, another person may decide to start a new life as a missionary to atone for engaging in morally unacceptable behavior, or yet another person may swear to never drive again after a car accident. Whereas these decisions are not bad and even virtuous in the first two examples, crisis workers should be directive in focusing clients on the resolution of the immediate crisis and strongly encourage postponing long-term decisions that have life changing implications.

> *CW:* I understand that it is difficult to make those first moves. That's why I am going to make these phone calls and get some information for you. This is not the rest of your life or getting married or moving to Samoa. It is seeing whether you can find some activities right now to take some of the loneliness away and replace what you thought crack would give you. So it is going to be up to you to contact these people. We are just looking for a little fun and recreation sans drugs. That is all we are about for right now.

2. <u>Make concrete plans</u>. The more plans are concrete, take into account client safety, provide a back up, and leave no loopholes, the more effective they tend to be. Plans that are imprecise and vague often are not completed. Crisis workers should help clients consider the issues of "what", "when", and "how" in the development of a plan. "What" concerns the actions that clients take to resolve a crisis, "when" involves the time these actions take place, and "how" includes the way the plans are to be accomplished. Crisis workers have the responsibility to help clients develop plans that address these three issues.

> *CL:* Thanks for the phone numbers. I'll give them a call in a couple of days.

> *CW:* Glad I could help. By the way, when are you going to call next week?

> *CL:* I don't know just sometime next week…when I get a chance.

> *CW:* Is there a day that is better than others?

> *CL:* I think Tuesday would be good. I can call them Tuesday.

> *CW:* What are you going to say?

Step 6- <u>Obtaining Commitment</u>

In crisis intervention, obtaining a commitment is particularly important as a way of moving a frozen client into action. The issue of client autonomy and control apply even more to the commitment stage because it does little good for the crisis worker to force clients to commit to do something when they do not have the resources to do so. Thus, gaining a commitment should be done as empathically and collaboratively as possible so the client doesn't wind up attempting to do something that is enforced on him or her by the crisis worker. If planning has been effectively done, the commitment step should be short, concise, and easily accomplished.

Obtaining Commitment – Rules of the Road

1. <u>Review plan</u>. As a session ends, the plan should be thoroughly reviewed with clients. A key element is having clients restate the plan in their own words. This process allows crisis workers to correct clients' interpretation of the plan and add parts of the plan that were left out.

> *CW:* So we're agreed that no matter how lonely things get during the weekend, before you decide to go find some dope you will call your sponsor in NA. Not having a phone in your apartment is not an excuse. You can call him from the convenience store. A busy signal or somebody using the phone at the convenience store will not be an excuse for not getting in contact with your support person. You'll stay at the convenience store until you can get through to them. If for any reason you cannot get through to your sponsor then you've agreed to call me no matter what time of the day or night. Again, a busy signal is not a reason for not calling me. Again, this is not a forever deal, this is just for the weekend. What did I just say?

> *CL:* I'm suppose to call my sponsor when I want to shoot up.

> *CW:* Yea, what else?

> *CL:* If the phone is busy I should keep trying...

2. <u>Establish responsibility</u>. Client commitment may be gained by a verbal agreement, a handshake, or a written contract, but however it is made, it must be clear that the client owns his or her part of the agreement and will follow through on it.

> *CW:* So are we agreed on that? Do we need to write it out or is a handshake your bond?

Summary

This first section has introduced you to a brief background and history of crisis intervention. You have been given an operational Triage Assessment Model used to assess for the severity of the crisis and a Six-step model used for crisis intervention with some "Rules of the Road" to help you as you start to interact with the scenarios in the CD. Section Two introduces you to nine strategies used with clients in crisis and also discusses tailoring these to clients' reactions.

Reflection Questions

1. Describe a crisis you have had in the pat year. How did you know this situation was a crisis and not an emergency or trauma?

2. Think about the time that you helped someone who was having a crisis. What steps in the systematic model do you remember using?

3. How do you think the Rules of the Road would have been helpful as you helped someone who was having a crisis?

References

Adler, A. (1958). What life should mean to you. New York: Putnam's Capricorn Books.

Baldwin, B. A. (1978). A paradigm for the classification of emotional crises: Implications for crisis intervention. *American Journal of Orthopsychiatry, 48,* 538–551.

Belkin, G. S. (1984). *Introduction to counseling* (2nd ed.). Dubuque, IA: William C. Brown.

Brammer, L. M. (1985). *The helping relationship: Process and skills* (3rd ed.). Englewood Cliffs, NJ: Prentice-Hall.

Callahan, J. (1994). Defining crisis and emergency. *Crisis, 15,* 164–171.

Callahan, J. (1998). Crisis theory and crisis intervention in emergencies. In P. M. Kleespies (Ed.), *Emergencies in mental health practices: Evaluation and management* (pp. 22-40). New York: Guilford Press.

Canter, L., & Canter, E. (1982). *Assertive discipline for parents.* Santa Monica, CA: Canter Associates.

Caplan, G. (1961). *An approach to community mental health.* New York: Grune & Stratton.

Caplan, G. (1964). *Principles of preventive psychiatry.* New York: Basic Books.

Carkhuff, R. R., & Berenson, B. G. (1977). *Beyond counseling and therapy* (2nd ed.). New York: Holt, Rinehart & Winston.

Cormier, W. H., & Cormier, L. S. (1991). *Interviewing strategies for helpers: Fundamental skills and cognitive behavioral interventions* (3rd ed.). Pacific Grove, CA: Brooks/Cole.

Cournoyer, B. R. (1996). Converging themes in crisis intervention, task-centered and brief treatment approaches. In A. R. Roberts (Ed.), *Crisis management and brief treatment* (pp. 3–15). Chicago: Nelson-Hall.

Distler, B. J. (1990). Reducing the potential for burnout. Paper presented at the Fourteenth Annual Convening of Crisis Intervention Personnel. Chicago.

Eisler, R. (1995). *Sacred pleasure: Sex, myth, and the politics of the body.* San Francisco: Harper-Collins.

Freudenberger, H. J. (1974). Staff burn-out. *Journal of Social Issues, 30,* 159-165.

Gilliland, B. E., & James, R. K. (1989). *Crisis intervention strategies and techniques* (1st ed.). Pacific Grove, CA: Brooks/Cole.

Glasser, W. (1976). *Positive addiction.* New York: Harper & Row.

James, R. K., & Gilliland, B. E. (2001). *Crisis intervention strategies and techniques* (4th ed.). Pacific Grove, CA: Brooks/Cole.

Kleespies, P. M., & Blackburn, E. J. (1998). The emergency telephone call. In P. M. Kleespies (Ed.), *Emergencies in mental health practices: Evaluation and management* (pp. 174-195). New York: Guilford Press.

Kleespies, P. M., Deleppo, J. D., Mori, D. L., & Niles, B. L. (1998). The emergency interview. In P. M. Kleespies (Ed.), *Emergencies in mental health practices: Evaluation and management* (pp. 41-74). New York: Guilford Press.

Kolski, T. D., Avriette, M., & Jongsma, A. E., Jr. (2001). *The crisis counseling and traumatic events treatment planner*. New York: John Wiley and Sons.

Kreidler, M. C., & England, D. B. (1990). Empowerment through group support: Adult women who are survivors of incest. *Journal of Family Violence, 5,* 35–41.

Maslach, C. (1982). *The cost of caring*. Upper Saddle River, NJ: Prentice-Hall.

McFarlane, A. C., & Yehuda, R. (1996). Resilience, vulnerability, and the course of posttraumatic reactions. In B. A. van der Kolk, A. C. McFarlane, & L. Weisaeth (Eds.), *Traumatic stress: The effects of overwhelming experience on mind, body, and society* (pp. 155-181). New York: Guilford Press.

Mc Raith, C. F. (1991, April). Coping with society's secret: Social support, job stress, and burnout among therapists treating victims of sexual abuse. Paper presented at the Fifteenth Annual Convening of Crisis Intervention Personnel. Chicago.

Myer, R. A. (2001). *Assessment for crisis intervention: A triage assessment model*. Pacific Grove, CA: Brooks/Cole.

Myer, R., Williams, R. C., Ottens, A. J., & Schmidt, A. E. (1992). A three-dimensional model for triage. *Journal of Mental Health Counseling, 14,* 137-148.

Pynoos, R. S., Steinburg, A. M., & Goenjian, A. (1996). Traumatic stress in childhood and adolescence: Recent developments and current controversies. In B. A. van der Kolk, A. C. McFarlane, & L. Weisaeth (Eds.), *Traumatic stress: The effects of overwhelming experience on mind, body, and society* (pp. 331–358). New York: Guilford Press.

Raphael, B., & Wilson, J. P. (2000). Introduction and overview: Key issues in the conceptualization of debriefing. In B. Raphael & J. P. Wilson (Eds.), *Psychological debriefing: Theory, practice, and evidence* (pp. 1-16). Cambridge, UK: Cambridge Press.

Rudd, M. D., Joiner, T. E., Jr., Jobes, D. A., & King, C. A. (1999). The outpatient treatment of suicidality: An integration of science and recognition of its limitations. *Professional Psychology: Research and Practice, 30,* 437– 446.

Sanchez, H. G. (2001). Risk factor for model suicide assessment and intervention. *Professional Psychology: Research and Practice, 32,* 351-358.

Salter, A. C. (1988). *Treating child sex offenders and victims: A practical guide*. Newbury Park, CA: Sage Publications.

Seely, M. F. (1997). The discreet role of the hotline. *Crisis, 18 (2),* 53-54.

Ursano, R. J., Grieger, T. A., & McCarroll, J. E. (1996). Prevention of posttraumatic stress: Consultation, training, and early treatment. In B. A. van der Kolk, A. C. McFarlane, & L. Weisaeth (Eds.), *Traumatic stress: The effects of overwhelming experience on mind, body, and society* (pp. 441– 462). New York: Guilford Press.

van der Kolk, B. S., & McFarlane, A. C. (1996). The black whole of trauma. In B. A. van der Kolk, A. C. McFarlane, & L. Weisaeth (Eds.), *Traumatic stress: The effects of overwhelming experience on mind, body, and society* (pp. 3–23). New York: Guilford Press.

Walker, L. E. (1989). *Terrifying love: Why women kill and how society responds.* New York: Harper & Row.

Watters, D. (1997). *A study of the reliability and validity of the Triage Assessment Scale.* Dissertation Abstracts.

SECTION TWO

Strategies and Levels of Intervention

This chapter describes nine strategies used in crisis intervention. The basic Core Listening and responding skills discussed in Section One are the foundation of these strategies. Following the discussion of the strategies, three levels of intervention will be described. These three levels of intervention allow crisis workers to customize and use the nine strategies to match the severity of clients' reactions. As strategies are discussed, we will indicate the reaction with which it is most often used. Further, we will indicate which of the six steps of the Gilliland and James Systematic Model for Crisis Intervention the strategy is utilizing. Finally, we will also identify types of clients for which the strategy may be more effective.

The case of Mary described in Figure 2.1 will be used to illustrate the use of the strategies and levels of intervention. Mary was seen by a psychologist during the first few days her son was admitted to the hospital in order to treat his leukemia. The crisis intervention services provided helped Mary regain a sense of equilibrium as she dealt with the medical issues related to her son's diagnosis and sorted through the meaning of this for her life. The case is a good example of complications that can be associated with a crisis.

Figure 2.1

Mary is a 32-year-old white female married nine years with one son, age seven, named Peter. She recently began work at a large, well-respected public relations firm, a job she had wanted since graduating college. Since receiving the job, Mary has worked on average 10 hours a day because she loves the work. She travels approximately 3 days a month and hopes to eventually become an account executive at the firm. Mary spends as much time with her son as possible given her new job. She enjoys participating with him in various social activities but recognizes that her free time is limited due to her work schedule. The relationship between Mary and her husband has become strained over the last year. Both are involved in their professional lives with their son being the primary connection between them. As a result of a routine yearly visit to the pediatrician, Peter was referred to the hospital for some blood tests. The pediatrician told Mary she was concerned about a couple of things but that it was probably nothing. The blood tests at the hospital confirmed that Peter has leukemia. Mary was told by the doctors at the hospital the situation was serious but that with proper treatment the chances of her son surviving were very good. Mary reacted in disbelief wondering how long it would be before her son died. Mary was referred to a psychologist who works at the hospital to help her as she tries to understand and help her son during this time.

Strategies

Each of the nine strategies can be used with affective, behavioral, or cognitive reactions to crisis although specific strategies may be used more often with certain reactions than others. For example, using a guidance strategy in connecting clients to community resources is primarily used to address behavioral rather than affective reactions to a crisis. Similarly, a catharsis strategy that helps clients come to grips with a loss would be used to address affective reactions more often than behavioral reactions.

While the intensity of each of the specific reactions may vary given the duration and kind of crisis, it is important to keep in mind that crises always involve affective, behavioral, and cognitive reactions. Clients will have varying degrees of reactivity in each of these three domains. However, all three domains must be addressed; otherwise the potential for long-term psychological problems is created. Therefore, we do not advise reliance on one strategy. We have found that in the course of crisis intervention, multiple strategies may be needed to help clients regain the sense of equilibrium and restore their pre-crisis level of functioning.

We do not know a formula for deciding which strategy to use, at what time, under which conditions, with what particular crisis. What we do know is that constant and ongoing assessment of the affective, behavioral, and cognitive status of the client is a critical factor in deciding what the crisis interventionist will do. Assessment overarches the James and Gilliland Six Step model (2001, p. 32) and it is of critical importance that the crisis worker continuously assesses a client and be ready to shift strategies immediately when conditions warrant.

We encourage you to notice that several Core Listening Skills are used in demonstrating each strategy. Seldom do we use Core Listening Skills singularly. Crisis intervention uses several Core Listening Skills in combination to achieve the goal of that strategy. Notice in each of the following exchanges how the crisis worker using several Core Listening Skills, at times within the same response, achieves the objective of the strategy. Following are the nine strategies.

Awareness

The crisis worker attempts to bring to conscious awareness warded off, denied, shunted, and repressed feelings, thoughts, and behaviors that freeze the client's ability to act in response to the crisis.

This strategy is particularly useful in the Listening phase or first three steps (Defining the Problem, Ensuring Client Safety, and Providing Support) of the Systematic Model. During these initial steps, clients may be so shocked that they have little, if any awareness, of what they are feeling, doing, or thinking. There are two typical groups of clients for whom this strategy is most helpful. First are those who depersonalize and are shocked into numbness by the crisis and are behaving in a robotic way, merely going through motions, which have little or no effect on the resolution of the crisis (Carlson, 1997). If and when these individuals talk about the crisis, it may be in a very mechanistic, reporter type way with little or any affect appropriate to the traumatic situation.

Second are clients who dissociate (Wagner & Linehan, 1998) from the crisis. They act as if they are not even in a crisis and everything is normal. It is as if these individuals are looking at the crisis from a viewing stand or a television set and it is not actually happening to them. Normal negative affective reactions such as grief, rage, and anger are completely submerged and are replaced by a "normal" range of feelings, behaviors, and thoughts that are entirely out of place in a very traumatic and abnormal situation. If these individuals do talk about their reactions, they may express them as if the crisis is happening to another person. In extreme and rare cases these clients enter into a state of fugue in which they may create an entirely new identity for themselves (van der Kolk, 1996a). Several of these cases were reported by the media almost one year after the September 11th terrorist attacks. With both groups, patience is important. Moving too fast in creating awareness may increase resistance and escalate the crisis.

In this exchange, Mary is not aware of her feelings or thoughts about the crisis. The crisis worker patiently moves Mary into awareness of these in such a manner as to allow Mary a sense of control.

MARY : (Voice has minimal inflection, almost monotone, shakes her head from side to side, with a blank look and tapping her fingers over and over.) It's just like I am going through the motions. I can't let this get me down. I've gotta be strong and go to work, act like nothing is happening. But it's like watching a soap opera, I can't believe it is really happening . . . . . he [Peter] is going to die…. It just isn't real.

CW : Sounds like you don't know what to feel right now. But mostly you seem scared.

MARY: (Grimaces and twists hands). I don't want to feel, maybe I am scared. But I keep asking myself, "Why is this happening right now? I've got such a good job."

CW: I get the feeling you may be angry. Can you say something about that?

MARY: (Surprised look on her face.) What do you mean, angry? I'm not sure about that, I can't be angry.

CW : Just take a minute and let's talk about it. It doesn't seem very fair this is happening to you. After all your life seemed to be going the way you wanted it to until Peter was diagnosed with Leukemia.

MARY : (Pace quickens. Voice inflection also increases and becomes more animated.) You've got that right. They [Doctors] said something about starting treatments immediately. I can't miss work. It is too important right now. I know my husband won't help.

CW : I can hear an edge in your voice, tell me about that.

MARY: What edge? I can't say what I really feel. He's my son and I love him. Why in the hell is this happening to me right now? Why did he get sick! It's just not fair! I am angry, but I shouldn't be! (Begins crying)

CW: You're right, it isn't fair. But it is okay to be angry.

The crisis worker senses Mary is overwhelmed by affective reactions including intense fear and anger. This reaction is compounded by her cognitive reactions of severe threat and transgression. These twin tidal waves of affective and cognitive duress translate into severe disequilibrium as she begins to sort through the meaning of her son's leukemia in her life. As a result she puts a severe behavioral constraint upon herself by pushing awareness away. However this constraint is minimally working as she is operating at the low end of "Marked Impairment" in the affective and cognitive domains. Notice how the crisis worker nudges Mary in small steps to awareness that she does have feelings about all that she is experiencing and how these are threatening. Also observe that the crisis worker does not force Mary out of the immobility to experience the feelings and thoughts, but only invites her to be aware of these. At the end of the dialogue the crisis worker reinforces and affirms Mary for her ability to acknowledge the warded off feelings.

Catharsis

The crisis worker provides a safe and accepting environment for clients to ventilate, air, expose, and bring forth feelings, thoughts, and behaviors generated by the crisis that may be perceived by clients as socially unacceptable or too psychologically hurtful to be shared. There are two primary reasons for promoting catharsis.

First, if left unexpressed, reactions to a crisis may become experienced as physical or psychological illnesses (Lindemann, 1944, 1956; Worden, 1991). They may become all consuming and constantly occupy the individual's feelings, behaviors, and thoughts (James & Gilliland, 2001) and effectively paralyze attempts to resume normal functioning. If kept submerged, these negative reactions may not only affect the individual's internal psychological processes but also have wide ranging toxic effects on interpersonal relationships as well (Miller & Iscoe, 1963).

Second, expression of reactions may help individuals increase their tolerance for the feelings and thoughts precipitated by the crisis that they have warded off as too threatening or unacceptable (van de Veer, 1998). Promoting catharsis is used to help clients express affective reactions throughout the Systematic Model. However, this strategy has specific utility in Step 1, "Defining the Problem" where a great deal of threatening affect and cognition about the crisis event may be occurring. Perhaps even more important to allowing and promoting catharsis is in Step 3, "Provide Support." By giving the client permission to cathart, the crisis worker validates the client's feeling and thinking as legitimate. Such validation may be critical to establishing trust and credibility, particularly when the client may see such a display of feelings and thoughts as a character defect or indeed, be given short shrift by significant others for such emotive displays.

Paradoxically, encouraging the expression of affective and cognitive reactions can backfire and should be done with caution (Myer, 2001). The reason for this prudence involves the need to regulate the expression of potentially volatile feelings and guard against emotions spiraling out of control (McFarlane & Yehuda, 1996). Client's who have lost control of their emotions and can no longer govern themselves need to be slowed down. The last thing the crisis worker wants is to make deep, reflective feeling responses with a client who is free wheeling emotionally. Such responses almost guarantee an *increase* in emotive behavior. This situation is particularly true for clients whose affective reaction is in the "Marked" to "Severe" range of the Triage Assessment Form. These clients already are experiencing a high level of disequilibrium and to encourage the expression of feelings might induce a state of hysteria or unrestrained anger. In such situations, crisis workers must control clients by using techniques to *limit* expression of feelings. Asking clients to take their time, take deep breaths, sit down, slow down talking and decrease the decibel level of their speech are all techniques to manage the expression of affect.

Cultural artifacts may play a large role in the crisis worker's efforts to allow catharsis to occur. In some cultures, expression of thoughts and feelings may be heavily sanctioned or even prohibited, while in other cultures it may be actively encouraged (Sue & Sue, 1999). For clients from cultures that inhibit the expression of emotions, crisis workers may offer the opportunity to express affective reactions, but not make implied demands that to "get better" clients must cathart. Instead, crisis workers must find culturally acceptable methods for the expression of these feelings. For example, anger may be expressed by physical activity such as in jogging or riding a bicycle. Sadness and grief may be alleviated by constructing memorials or engaging in philanthropic or charitable activities that relate to the crisis. Creative activities such as writing, drawing, carving, sculpting and other art mediums can also be used to express emotions that result from a crisis. These activities allow clients to express emotions while not necessarily verbalizing them.

For clients from cultures that advocate catharsis, care must also be taken not to license hysteria. Wild, unbridled expression of feelings may have ramifications for both client and worker safety. As we shall see, with Mary, her belief that she needs to be in control prevents the expression of feelings.

CW: Can you tell me more about what you are feeling?

MARY: I don't know… if I get started I may not be able to stop. I just can't let that happen.

CW: I don't understand. What makes you say you can't let that happen?

MARY: (Said sarcastically) I have to be strong, I can't turn into a blubbering idiot. That would scare Peter. And besides I won't give my husband the satisfaction.

CW: Wait a minute, I don't understand you won't give your husband the satisfaction.

MARY: Absolutely. If I come apart he'll tell me to quit work because "Women can't handle work and family at the same time" so he says. What the hell does he know?

CW: Let me understand this. Because he believes women can't handle work and family that means you can't have feelings.

MARY: (Pause) Sounds stupid when you say it like that (looks down as her eyes tear up). But I've got to work this out, my feelings only get in the way. I am so pissed with his macho attitudes. I've got a job too, and a good one….. And besides poor Peter….he needs me to be strong..... So I can't have feelings because his father is such an ass. (Voice level increases in pitch and loudness.)

CW: Sounds like you have a lot on your shoulders. Your husband and Peter aren't here. With me you can have feelings.

MARY: (Looks up and makes eye contact.) That's easy to say...... I really want to, but I'm so scared.

CW: Tell me about being scared.

MARY: (Pause and begins sobbing) I'm so scared. I can't lose my job. What if Peter dies? I've already lost my husband... (Continues crying).

CW: (Reaches out and gently touches Mary's shoulder). That does sound scary. What scares you the most?

MARY: (Continues crying and pauses before responding)...I know this sounds awful, but right now losing my job sounds the worst.

CW: What makes you say that?

MARY: (Looks up and sighs) I don't really mean that, but I think that sometimes. Of course if Peter dies I'll...I don't know what I would do.

CW: Seems pretty hard to figure out all that you are feeling right now, being scared and angry at the same time. I will be with you every step of the way and we can get through this.

MARY: Thanks.

In this exchange, Mary initially expresses her need to maintain rigid control over her emotions. Through a series of open-ended leads, restatements, and owning statements by the crisis worker, Mary begins to talk about her dilemma. As she does so, a number of reactions appear. The first is her anger at her husband. As the crisis worker reflects her feelings, deeper more unacceptable feelings emerge. These feelings go beyond her anger about her husband. Although she is fearful of Peter dying, Mary is also fearful of losing her job. The full impact of the crisis and her emotional reactions are beginning to emerge. She expresses remorse at having these feelings but with a nonjudgmental open-ended question, the crisis worker encourages Mary to express her feelings.

Gently touching Mary provides a concrete emotional anchor between her and the crisis worker. This allows Mary to safely disclose her feelings knowing the crisis worker will not abandon or judge her. Fear of being alone is a critical issue for Mary. The relationship between Mary and her husband provides little to no comfort. Now Mary faces losing Peter whom she loves. At a deeper level of being, she now wonders if she is losing her career. Openly acknowledging these feelings as real and legitimate is extremely threatening to Mary.

To encourage catharsis, the crisis worker moves carefully and patiently from Mary's denial of her affective reaction. Using open-ended leads, restatements, summary clarifications and owning statements about the worker's confusion, the cultural barrier of gender is overcome. The worker then moves into deeper emotional responses by probing Mary's dilemma. Finally, the crisis worker provides support by physically connecting with the client by touching her shoulder and verbally stating that he will see her through the crisis.

Validation

The crisis worker attempts to validate that the clients' reactions are appropriate, normal, customary, and expressed within culturally acceptable limits given the kind, type, and duration of the crisis provided these are not harmful psychologically, physically, or morally to self or others.

This strategy is primarily used to validate clients' affective reactions, but on occasion is used to support behavioral and cognitive reactions as well. Providing validation and assurance is utilized throughout the Systematic Model, but is particularly useful in Steps One through Three (Problem Exploration, Safety, and Support). In these steps clients often disclose they are unsure and doubtful of their reactions to the crisis. They often fear that they are going crazy. Questions such as "I'm not crazy am I" or "Do you think other people feel this way" are not unusual for clients who need their affective reactions validated. Clients needing support for behavioral and cognitive reactions express similar concerns. Statements such as "I wanted to do something but couldn't move" or "I wasn't able to drive by the place where the accident took place" may be expressed when looking for support of behavioral reactions. An example of a cognitive reaction for which a client needs validation is the expression of loss over an object. The client may say "I shouldn't be missing the *object* that much, but I just can't seem to help myself." Clients may also think they are losing their minds because the onslaught of data they are trying to handle is unimaginable and overwhelming (Matsakis, 1992). "It's like I can't think straight any more, it just gets in this big rats nest of thoughts that are all jumbled up. Maybe I have Alzheimer's."

Others question the legitimacy of the emotional reaction to the crisis and either discount, deny, or hide their reaction (Kleespies, Deleppo, Mori, & Niles, 1998). "I am a good Christian. I have never hated anyone. How can I be having these feelings? I've got to stop this. This isn't right." At times, the strength of the reaction shocks clients to the point they try to minimize or hold in the feelings. Generally speaking, these clients want to reduce discomfort by disregarding or restraining the expression of the reactions. Statements by these clients tend to be similar to "I have everything under control" or "No need to worry about me; things are just fine." Validating strategies can help clients overcome these resistances by making it okay to have feelings about the crisis, regardless of the intensity and assuring them that their reactions are within a range of experience that is common for the crisis and that, in fact, they are not crazy.

Clients may also experience the need for validation as they start to take their first tentative steps toward tackling the problems in Step Four, Examining Alternatives; Five, Planning; and Six, Commitment. Clients are often so paralyzed behaviorally and cognitively by the crisis that they now question everything they do and think. "Is this right? Should I stay or go? Is it better to tell him or not? Nothing like this ever happened before so I don't have any earthly idea what to do."

Clients may be reticent about seeking validation and support because until the crisis, they were masters of their own destinies. Seeking validation and support may be construed to be a sign of weakness. "If I seek support or ask for validation, I am a wimp. They'll think I can't cut it anymore, and they will be right!" In each of the foregoing cases, crisis workers need to validate that timidity and hesitancy in the face of a chaotic and absolutely new dilemma is common and does not mean the person is unequal to the task.

However, concomitant with this strategy and a problem that often arises for clients who need validation is dependence (Baldwin, 1979). Dependency is a problematic byproduct of much crisis intervention, particularly when validating clients. The simple fact of the matter is that many times clients do need to be dependent on crisis workers (Hobbs, 1984). In these situations, clients' reactions are usually in the marked to severe range in at least one of the domains of the Triage Assessment Form. Clients whose reactions are at this level are unable to shield themselves from the pressures of day-to-day living and rally any type of coping skills. Crisis workers should allow these clients the dependence they need until they are able to reestablish the capacity to cope with life on a day-to-day basis. However, often we have seen crisis workers become trapped and fall into the role of a surrogate parent when clients become dependent. The result is that crisis workers are frustrated and angry that they have gotten themselves in position that they now feel they are responsible for the client forever. If this situation develops, crisis workers should as quickly as is appropriate wean clients from the dependence (Valent, 1998). Easier said than done, the fine line between validating and supporting a client when necessary and creating life long dependency is one of the major reasons that all crisis workers need on going clinical supervision and periodic debriefings. As strong, self-sufficient, and capable as Mary is, she faces these same issues.

MARY: The doctors say Peter will be fine. I want to believe that, I have to believe that. I don't have to worry, the treatments are working, I can get back to work.

CW: You say you're fine, but the way you say that it seems… well, I am not convinced. Saying I'm fine will somehow make everything okay when it is anything but fine. If I were in the position you are in, I would not be fine by a long shot. I'd be scared out of my wits putting the life of my child in someone else's hands.

MARY: You're not a mother. How could you know what it is like to carry a child for 9 months.

CW: Whether I am a mother or not, I believe that every person, you included, would have every right to be scared in this situation.

MARY: Sometimes all this becomes so much it's like an avalanche. Just burying me and suffocating me. I ought not worry so much, Peter has great doctors…But it is like part of me is gone (Tears come into her eyes and hands start to wring uncontrollably).

CW: If you love and care for someone that much, why wouldn't you feel that way? If my child was facing death I would certainly feel that way.

MARY: Maybe. But I have just got to stop having these feelings. I am out-of-control. I think maybe I am going nuts sometimes.

CW: You are not going nuts. You're having a very typical reaction to a bad experience. If I brought ten other people in here under the same circumstances, they would all feel the same way and think they were going nuts too. None of them would be nuts. They might react in different ways too, but that would not be nuts either. They would be reacting in a normal way to an abnormal situation.

There is nothing magical or difficult about the use of this strategy. Over and over, the crisis worker constantly validates, supports, and reinforces the client that it is okay to have these reactions. Using a broken record/CD technique, the crisis worker patiently reinforces again and again that what the client is experiencing is normal. The same procedure is used as the client attempts to plan how to take action.

MARY: But I feel so all alone and I can't stop thinking about what might happen.

CW: Can you talk about this with anyone?

MARY: (In a meek tentative voice). I've kinda thought about talking with my sister. She always was able to listen, but I don't know. What would she think if I told her that unless my husband starts helping out, I'm going to tell him to leave?

CW: I don't know, what would she think?

MARY: (Laughs). She'd probably say, you should have done that long ago. You can bet she wouldn't be surprised. But now with Peter being sick and my job...(Voice trails off.)

CW: So she would probably understand and support you.

MARY: I guess, pretty much.

CW: So once you look at it closely talking with her is a good plan. It sounds like a good idea. When are you going to call her up? I believe this will work.

When in crisis, clients do not always hear something the first time it is said. Crisis workers may need to repeat something several times before clients are able to hear the message. In the process the crisis worker also points out that while Mary's reactions are typical, each person reacts in his or her own individual way to a crisis. Making this type of statement is important to help Mary not compare her reaction with the reactions of others. The need for this type of statement arises out of Mary's apparent comparison of her sanity with the sanity of others. Again this support helps Mary understand that she is having a common experience to the crisis. Overall the crisis worker's responses accomplish two seemingly dissimilar goals. First, the crisis worker authenticates Mary's feelings as being idiosyncratic to her. That is, while others may be sympathetic and empathic no one can experience the crisis as Mary does. Second, the crisis worker also helps Mary to see that her reactions are not unusual and that everyone would react in a similar fashion given a comparable situation. The result is that Mary experiences relief and allows the intervention process to progress.

Expansion

The crisis worker engages in activities to broaden, open-up, and increase clients' tunnel vision, restricted affect, perception, and interpretation of the crisis so that other affective and cognitive views and behavioral options may be considered.

Many times, clients in crisis will fall into a whirlpool that causes their affective, behavioral, and cognitive responses to become tighter and tighter and severely limit their ability to adapt to the crisis. Responses and options become less and less as the client engages in ever more narrowing functioning in an attempt to control the crisis (Naugle & Follette, 1998). This strategy is primarily used to help clients expand affective and cognitive reactions to the crisis in Steps One: Defining the Problem, and cognitive and behavioral responses in Step Four: Examine Alternatives and Step Five: Make Plans.

Restriction of cognition and subsequently the constriction of both affective and behavioral responses follow very closely Ellis' (1973) ABC model which believes that client catastrophize and propel themselves further and deeper into the crisis because of their irrational beliefs (B) about the event (A) and suffer even more adverse consequences (C). This black and white, all or none "mustabatory" thinking, as Ellis calls it, has high reinforcing capabilities and can quickly build a chain of illogical inferences into catastrophic dimensions. Once clients are locked into this irrational mode of operation, they put on psychological blinders that limit their perception of the environment to a tunnel view that includes only the crisis. Their attempts at a crisis solution generally degrade to one or two behavioral solutions that are not effective. Yet, they continue to recycle these behaviors with even less effectiveness.

A client who has just been jilted attempts to recapture his lost love by sending flowers, then chocolates, then designer clothing, and then diamonds. While the product is different, the method is the same, and the outcome, rejection, is the same. The only difference is that the price of the gifts escalates. The very fact that the reason for the rejection in the first place may have had to do with the client attaching a "price tag" to the relationship is never recognized. Expansion helps clients to start understanding such environmental cues and offering new perspectives on the crisis. If the jilted boyfriend starts to perceive he can't buy love and affection, but rather needs to start paying attention to his girlfriend's thoughts and feelings, and further decides that she *might* love him for who he is when he is with her and not that she *must* love him because of what he buys her, he has broadened his cognitive horizons and in the process has created new behavior adaptations for himself.

Not only are people in crisis often times not able to generate new and different behaviors, they may also forget behaviors they have used in the past that have been effective for them in similar instances. Under normal circumstances, most people are able to understand environmental cues to help them perceive the meaning of events. However, when in crisis, this ability is compromised and people misread and/or misinterpret cues (Shalev, 1996; van der Kolk, 1996b). By misreading or misinterpreting the environment, clients' beliefs are constricted, they make more and more irrational statements about the event, and their response is to engage in narrower, more maladaptive emotional attitudes and behavioral responses. In a sense, clients paint themselves into a semantic and belief system corner. They may not even acknowledge there are other interpretations of the event. Such clients are difficult to work with because they see only one way to resolve the crisis. They are "Yes butters." They may agree grudgingly that there may be other options but then discount the option by saying, "Yes, but that is not true for me." For this group of clients, expansion points out contradictions in their perceptions by inviting them to try out different points of view.

A high school student who moves to Florida was a champion speed skater on her Minnesota high school team and received a great deal of admiration and recognition. She was also on the debate team and played first chair trombone in the school band. However, since there is no speed skating team within two thousand miles of her in Orlando, she is depressed and disconsolate and constantly threatens to run away "up north" or bitterly complains how her parents have forsaken her. She becomes so consumed with the loss of her skating that she becomes more and more depressed, her grades fall to failing and she becomes suicidal. She is completely oblivious to the fact that there is an excellent high school band that is always short of that rare commodity, a good trombone player, and an opportunity to join the debate team when the speech teacher gets a letter from her teacher in International Falls. Further, because she is an over all excellent athlete who has been a pretty fair recreational tennis player (her former school did not have tennis as a sport) she completely forsakes the excellent coaching and tennis facilities at the school. If her new school counselor is able to jar her out of her endless feedback loop of catastrophizing over the loss of her skating, and can expand her restricted affect of what brings joy to her life, and get her to see that many of her old behavioral skills and abilities are still in place and readily available with some minor adaptations, then the client's tailspin will end. As we will see with Mary, expansion of affective responses and behavioral repertoires about a crisis often means vigorously confronting a client's irrational beliefs about it.

> MARY: You just don't get it do you? I don't have a choice. I must go to work, I can't give up my job!

> CW: You're right, I don't get it. Explain it to me one more time how this MUST be the only way to do that.

> MARY: (Forceful voice and making direct eye contact. Rate of speech rapid.) Look, I worked long and hard to get this job. Now they [managers at work] are starting to notice me. Just last week Dave [Immediate Manager] let me know that his boss likes the work I am doing.

> CW: I guess I don't understand, they are in control of you?

> MARY: Control me my ass, I have to do what I have to do.

> CW: I still don't understand. Look at it from my perspective.

> MARY: What do you mean?

CW: What I see is that you are reacting to them. Because they say something about you, you have no choice but to work harder. Who is in control?

MARY: Me, of course.

CW: Then why are you letting them dictate the time you spend with Peter?

MARY: I can choose what I want to do, they can't make me do anything. I can be with Peter at the hospital any time I want.

CW: Ohhhh. So you DO have a choice in this.

MARY: Yeah, I can choose what I want.

CW: So you do have other options. What might they be?

MARY: (Grudgingly). Well, maybe! I guess I can talk with Dave and see about checking out a laptop to use while Peter is getting his treatments…

CW: Have you asked about the Family Leave Policy?

MARY: I thought about it, but I haven't done anything. I'm not sure I'm ready to do that.

CW: Okay, anything else you might do to take control?

MARY: Maybe I could talk to Dave planning my travel more in advance or doing more conference calls. Hell, they would like that because it would save money.

In this exchange Mary's perception about the hassles she is receiving at work is extremely narrow. As she begins, Mary is adamant about what she must do. Because Dave [Immediate Boss] said her work is being noticed she must work even harder. The crisis worker must carefully work to move Mary from this inflexible position. To accomplish this goal, the crisis worker must confront the stance Mary has taken without alienating her. Mary believes she has no choices but to be at work more. The crisis worker uses a series of open ended and closed questions that constantly push against Mary's restrictive view of her options. The worker also makes a series of owning statements that clearly state the worker's objective, more rational understanding of the situation and are designed to make Mary look harder at her options. The crisis worker leads Mary to the conclusion she has options available, even if she only grudgingly agrees and "Yes buts" the crisis worker. It is patient, gentle, yet dogged confrontation by the crisis worker that the client does have choices that enables this new, somewhat broader perspective to emerge. At this point, the crisis worker can help Mary brainstorm additional ways to respond to the crisis.

Focus

The crisis worker attempts to qualify, narrow, and downsize clients' all encompassing, catastrophic, interpretations and perceptions of the crisis event into more specific, realistic, manageable components and options.

Emphasizing focus is the opposite of expansion. For some individuals, crises unleash a cyclone of colliding feelings, thoughts, and behaviors that may threaten their own or others safety (Novaco & Chemtob, 1998). They are not able to draw a distinction between the crisis and the rest of their life. Often these clients will make universal, sweeping statements such as "My life is over since I found out my spouse is having an affair" or "I'll never get another job since I got fired." The goal of focusing is to interrupt the out-of-control and hysterical responding of those clients. This strategy is primarily used to address cognitive reactions that are not based in objective fact or the reality of the situation. Much like clients who have too narrow a perception of the crisis, clients who have too broad a response to the crisis and let it flood into all aspects of their lives are explained by Ellis' (1973) theory about irrational beliefs. In attempting to create more calm and rational focus within the individual, Dryden (1984) promotes the use of cold or warm, rather than hot cognitions.

Cold cognitions of an event are generally descriptions, observations and nonevaluative inferences about it. "My husband died suddenly. There are a lot of financial details to take care of and I am going to need some help." Warm cognitions emphasize preferences and nonpreferences rather than necessities and absolutes. "My husband died suddenly. It was a shock. I don't like having to deal with all the financial details but I guess I am going to have to. I will need some help." Warm cognitions may have mild to intense emotions, but as long as they indicate preferences they are not hot cognitions. Hot cognitions emphasize demands, commands, and absolutes. "MY GOD! MY HUSBAND IS DEAD. I KNOW NOTHING ABOUT OUR FINANCES. WHAT WILL I EVER DO? I CAN'T LIVE WITH THIS PAIN AND FEAR. I MUST DO SOMETHING NOW!" Hot cognitions are usually laced with emotional demand statements that take the form of overgeneralizing, catastrophizing, magnification, non sequiturs, personalizing, labeling, and all-or-none thinking (Ellis, 1984). It is these hot cognitions with which focusing is mainly concerned.

This strategy is used in all steps of the Systematic Model with clients who have been overwhelmed by the crisis but is probably most important in Step 2, Safety, where such behavior may have lethal consequences. Using this strategy also helps clients who want to make long-term decisions in the midst of a crisis. Making long-term decisions based on reactions to a crisis is generally not advisable and generally has adverse consequences for the client. The foregoing example of the sudden death of a spouse who made all the financial decisions and who left no will or request for how the remains were to be taken care of is a classic example for potentially bad long term decisions as a result of hot cognitions about the crisis event. The bereaved, out-of-control spouse may be very vulnerable to suggestions by others who may not have her best interests at heart.

The key to focusing is helping clients regulate and modify their perceptions while not being critical of them. One of the most common problems in crisis intervention is cooling off hot cognitions that pour out from the crisis event and flood multiple aspects of the client's environment.

MARY: (Agitated and twisting his hands uncontrollably). I have been really thinking about all this. Peter is going to die. Having leukemia means only one thing. He is going to die. All the doctors can do is prolong his life a little. Then I will have nothing, my husband is basically gone, my friends won't know what to say.

CW: You sound awfully SURE of yourself… Peter dying, your husband not caring, and what did you say…Your friends won't know what to say.

MARY: "Sure" is not near the right word. IT WILL HAPPEN. It is bound to happen. No one knows what to say. They're all stupid. You know, a friend from church came to see me yesterday. She asked if Peter caught the leukemia from me.

CW: You mean absolutely all your friends are stupid because they say dumb things.

MARY: I am in this by myself. My job is down the drain, my marriage is the pits, Peter will die. Nothing is going right. Now my friends are wondering what I did to cause Peter to get sick. I'd just as soon get it over with. As long is Peter is sick, I have no life.

CW: What do you mean get it over with? You sound like you are giving up.

MARY: No, I'm not giving up and I'm not going to stop Peter's treatments if that is what you mean. But I thought about it.

CW: You thought about it, I don't understand?

MARY: (Raises voice) LIKE I SAID, I don't have a life.

CW: No anything, you mean nothing at all, absolutely nothing, nil, zilch, nada, zero!

MARY: (Exasperated and agitated). That's right, nothing. Why are you asking me these idiotic questions?

CW: I still don't understand. You are living in a void. No family, no church, no faith, no job, no jogging, no lunches with your sister, no playing the music, no anything.

MARY: (Big sigh.) Well no, I can still go to church, my family has been helpful, and God hasn't abandoned me. The people at work have been supportive thus far. I suppose I could find time to jog or at least take a walk.

CW: (Summarizing cooler cognitions and comparing them to the client's hot ones). Let me get this straight. God or your family hasn't abandoned you and you still can go to church. Your co-workers understand. What else…oh you can take a walk while Peter is sleeping. Didn't you just say none of those people, your friends or family would give one tinker's damn about you, just suffer by yourself, abandoned by all?

MARY: Well, no. That's nuts. I do have friends in those places, and my family would love me no matter what.

CW: (Asking for confirmation). Say that again. The part about still having friends and support.

MARY: (Quiet voice) I do have friends there. Is that what you want me to say? But what's the use. I won't have a job.

CW: (Stating a factual cold cognition) You mean you were fired.

MARY: (Calmer, but still hanging on to the hot cognition). Well no, actually they said I could work my schedule around the treatments. Dave [Immediate Manager] said he is going to give me a cell phone.

CW: (Summarizing and asking for more cold facts). Give you a cell phone?

MARY: (Somewhat sheepishly). He said only he would know the number and just in case a question came up about my accounts that he couldn't answer he would call me.

In this exchange Mary states an all or nothing attitude. She expresses the view that she is alone and no one cares enough to be supportive. Mary also thinks because one friend is seeming to blame her for Peter's illness, all her friends will. While she may be labeled by some people, she will certainly not be labeled by all people in that manner. This type of catastrophizing is common for clients in crisis. The task of the crisis worker is to move Mary from the perception that all is lost to a view that is less absolute. Through the series of exchanges the crisis worker carefully helps Mary see that her interpretation of the crisis is not based on fact but rather her over generalizing and magnification of the event. The crisis worker is even able to get

Mary to list the ways people have been supportive and with her job, have even gone to great lengths to be helpful.

Guidance

The crisis worker provides information, referral, and direction in regards to clients obtaining assistance from specific external resources and support systems.

Guiding strategies direct clients to resources that will help to resolve the crisis. The goal is to funnel clients to organizations, charities, programs, and institutions that are able to be helpful. In a sense, crisis workers are information kiosks; that is they are knowledgeable of community resources needed by clients. As such, the strategy is used almost exclusively to respond to clients' behavioral reactions. In the Systematic Model, the strategy is used primarily in Step Four, "Examining Alternatives" and Five, "Making a Plan". This strategy is particularly beneficial for clients who are unaware of available community resources. For example, victims of violent crimes may not be aware that in many communities non-profit agencies specializing in working with victims exist. In this situation, crisis workers would guide clients to access this resource in order to aid in the resolution of the crisis. Statements like "Have you tried _____ agency" or "This agency may be able to help, the phone number is _____". We strongly encourage crisis workers and agencies to keep a list of agencies available. Ideally the list should contain an agency's name, contact person, phone number, services provided, fees (if applicable), and other information that could conceivably be of use in crisis situations.

The simple fact of the matter is that in a crisis most people may have very little idea of what resources are available to them. To assume some client centered, nondirective role where the client has to figure out who or what the resources are at this juncture is patently ridiculous. As we stated previously, dependence can become a problem with clients needing guidance. Some clients learn quickly to manipulate crisis workers to do things. We encourage you to be cautious and continually assess clients' needs if dependence becomes an issue. But the bottom line is that crisis workers generally should have the kinds of referral resources at hand that clients in crisis need and they should not be hesitant about bringing them into operation.

> *MARY:* Do you know of anyplace that I can get help with handling all this?

> *CW:* I'm glad you asked. I was going to tell you anyway. The "Caring Place" is an agency that has support groups for parents whose children have cancer.

> *MARY:* Cancer, I can't stand the sound of that word.

> *CW:* That is tough to hear. The "Caring Place" has groups several times a week plus they have a lot of information.

> *MARY:* I don't know. I have to think about it. I'm not sure I'm ready for that.

> *CW:* You might try the American Cancer Society. They even have a web site. As a matter of fact, I have a list of web sites that might be helpful.

> *MARY:* Thanks. Maybe that wouldn't be too bad an idea, looking at the web sites. I feel so dumb, why didn't I think of that?

The crisis worker simply reminds Mary of the resources that are available and provides information. Mary's last statement is not unusual for clients in this situation. Clients often overlook obvious resources and merely need to be reminded that there are resources out there. As such, the crisis worker provides several resources and does not press Mary to contact the "Caring Place".

Mobilization

The crisis worker attempts to activate and marshal both the internal resources of the client and to find and use external support systems to help generate coping skills and problem solving abilities.

Mobilization is used exclusively to address clients' behavioral reactions. Mobilization is used in Step One, "Problem Definition", Step Four, "Generating Alternatives", Step Five, "Making Plans", and Step Six, "Obtaining Commitment", of the Systematic Model. It is in these steps that clients generally need a helping hand to initiate movement toward resolving the crisis. Early in Step One, Problem Definition, the crisis worker may compliment clients for being proactive and mobile with the idea in mind that this will reinforce them and make them even more mobile. "I know it really took some courage to pick up the phone and call in today. Being in a battering situation is scary." When looking for alternatives in Step Five and planning in Step Six the crisis worker may use the client's internal resources "What have you done in past situations like this?" or "Even though you never talked to the guidance counselor in your old high school, I personally know Mrs. James in your new one, and she is pretty knowledgeable about study skills. What could it cost you besides a little time? It would be at least a step towards getting back on track academically."

Mobilization is utilized with client's whose reactions to crisis range from mild to severe. Typically, however, it is most useful with client's whose reactions fall into the mild and moderate ranges because these clients only need assistance in reactivating problem-solving techniques. Crisis workers will at times serve as a cheerleader for clients. Early in the intervention, during Step One of Problem Solving, the crisis worker should praise the client for being proactive and mobile. "I know it really took some courage to pick up the phone and call in today. Being in a battering situation is scary." Stuhlmiller and Dunning (2000) refer to the client's ability to access and activate (mobilize) inner resources and remain healthy after stressful encounters as salutogenisis. Salutogenisis speaks to the client's positive outlook or approach to life, as opposed to a pathogenic or sick view. When the client is able to experience stress as coherent, manageable, and meaningful, their coping abilities increase, as well as their sense of health and well-being.

A specific group of clients who benefit from a mobilization strategy are those whose behaviors exacerbate the crisis rather resolve it. These clients, to one degree or another, are mobilized, but engaged in unhealthy or destructive attempts to resolve the crisis. This situation can be due to the severity of the reactions (van der Kolk, 1996b) or to clients taking on a "I am too sick to do it" role (Violanti, 2000). With these clients, crisis workers must redirect efforts toward healthy, constructive behaviors. Again, attempts to elicit dependency are likely to arise with clients experiencing mobilization problems. Mary has decided to talk with the doctor about a second opinion and alternative treatments. Notice how she tries to get the crisis worker to do this for her. This situation is not unusual in a medical setting since many people have been taught not to question doctors.

MARY: (Breaking out in a sweat). I can't do this myself.

CW: What makes you say that?

MARY: (Avoiding the question) Why don't you just talk with the doctor. You have my permission to do it. I'll even write it out.

CW: I'm surprised to hear that given everything we have talked about during the past few days. You have role played this with me and know what you are going to say. You have it down pat.

MARY: But it is not enough. I know you can fix things. I trust you.

CW: You want the easy way out.

MARY: Not really, but I can't do it.

CW: I'm sure you can. Now remember what you would say.

MARY: I guess I would first apologize for being so angry.

CW: That's a good start. What next?

MARY: (Avoids crisis worker). I don't know. I can't remember.

CW: Something about getting a second opinion and wanting the best treatment for Peter.

MARY: Yeah, okay. But what will I say?

CW: What do you need to say?

MARY: I know you know a lot about leukemia but is there another doctor that I can talk with?...Maybe I could ask if he is telling me everything and ask about other treatments? I still don't know if I can do this by myself.

CW: I wonder if maybe you could ask your sister if she is willing to be with you.

MARY: Good idea, she would do that.

CW: Let's make a list of specific questions. I want you to take this pad and write each one down. You may also want to have your sister write down what the doctor says. Take them one at a time.

Clients who are immobilized have to be led at times step by step through a sequence of activities that will approximate them to the total goal. Such steps need to be discrete, specific, and concrete so that clients can role play or practice if they need to do so. Notice that the crisis worker constantly reinforces Mary as he not only attempts to mobilize her plan but mobilize her courage as well. This at times may seem like hand holding, and somewhat childish, but just like the lion in <u>The Wizard of Oz</u>, clients need to find their "heart" and their courage after a traumatic event.

Ordering

The crisis worker methodically helps clients classify and categorize problems so as to prioritize and sequentially attack the crisis in a logical and linear manner.

Implementing order helps clients slow down, take a step back, and use sound, common sense to understand and deal with the crisis. This strategy is used primarily to assist clients in the resolution of cognitive reactions, but can be used to help clients organize behavioral reactions. Implementing order is used throughout the Systematic Model with clients whose perceptions and/or behaviors are not well thought-out or impulsive. On the TAF, the severity of reactions of clients for whom this strategy is helpful ranges from mild to severe. A specific group of clients that benefit from implementing order are those who have not had enough time to process the crisis. The closeness in time skews their perceptions and prevents them from being reasonable with respect to the crisis. When clients are cognitively suffering from loss, transgression, or threat, working methodically through the needs hierarchy on the Cognitive dimension of the TAF is one of the best ways to slow thinking down, prioritize needs, and provide a return to equilibrium. Similarly, when clients are behaviorally approaching, avoiding, or being immobile in a maladaptive way on the TAF, methodically helping clients order their behaviors can be one of the most effective methods available of returning homeostasis to the client. Witness the crisis worker's initial meeting with Mary.

MARY: (almost hyperventilating) I need some help...The whole world has turned up side down . I found out my son has leukemia...and I don't know what to do, the doctors say he'll be fine...but I think I need to tell somebody...and I need to call work...How much is this going to cost?...Should I call the insurance?...What if I did something wrong?...I don't know but I am going nuts I think and...

CW: (Raising hands in a T sign). You are going too fast for me! Take a deep breath and slow down a bit. I understand there are a number of things going on in your life about something that has you terribly unsettled right now. I want to hear what those are, but need for you to slow down. We have time. We have plenty of time. Do you understand that?

MARY: (Nods her head and gulps some air).

CW: Good, excellent! Now take another deep breath and just let the air slowly out of you and relax. Good! Now I want you to take one piece. Not necessarily the biggest piece of this problem. Just one piece, understand (Client nods) Good. Now take that piece and just write it down on this piece of paper and let me look at it. You could probably tell me, but write it down so you have some time to think about it. Just take your time and write it down. We will get to everything you need to tell me, but just one at a time, okay.

MARY: (Writes down statement which reads): Peter was just diagnosed with leukemia and they want to start treatments tomorrow.

CW: That does sound serious and sounds like you have to make some decisions.

Many times in the initial, opening stages of a problem clients have so many things going on that they become a whirling, tumbling mass of confused, jumbled pieces of information salad. They spill this information out making it extremely difficult for crisis workers to follow what is being said. By using a broken record/CD technique of slowly telling the client over and over that there is plenty of time, the message hopefully sinks through the manic thinking and manic behavior to slow down the client's cartwheeling thinking. By forcing the client to write down one problem only, the client has to stop, think, prioritize, and put down a coherent thought.

Using a Maslowian Needs Hierarchy approach as is illustrated in the Cognitive section of the TAF, the crisis worker attempts to take care of basic, survival needs first. Safety and survival are always a top priority. Suffice it to say that very little resolution of inter- and intra personal problems gets done with survivors who have just gone through a tornado until they have some food, clothing and shelter. In this situation, Mary has several decisions to make quickly. The doctors have said they want to initiate treatment for Peter's leukemia the next day. Mary also needs to make decisions about work. The crisis worker creates a situation that forces Mary to slow down. Slowing down is just what Mary needs to stop the merry-go-round of thoughts she is experiencing.

When we move to the Alternatives and Planning stages the same problem may occur as clients are overwhelmed with choices, many of which will require new behaviors and divergent thinking. These new thoughts and behaviors may become very threatening to the client. This situation takes place several days after Peter began treatment. The crisis worker again must put a brake on Mary's swirling thought processes.

MARY: (Engaging in a running free flight of ideation). There is so much I need to do. I have to fly to Chicago next week for work. But I need to get a presentation done. I should call the benefits office at work. I need to call the church and let them know what is going on. I almost forgot about having lunch tomorrow with my team. I have the chicken out for dinner this evening and I have to get my hair cut for my trip…

CW: What we are going to do is take a deep breath and S…L….O…W down. Right now you need to do one thing and one thing only, Okay? First, you need to decide if you want to make the trip next week. Get out your list of reasons of "Yes" and "NO" you made yesterday. I don't think I heard any of those reasons coming out. So, look at them. Right now as you study those reasons what do you want to do?

MARY: (Studies list). Well, I guess I should go to the meeting but I am worried about Peter being sick…The meeting is important.

CW: Sounds like you are beginning to think through this some. How can you get information updates on Peter's treatment next week if you go to Chicago?

The crisis worker does not attempt to respond to the verbal barrage or the panic of the client. Instead, the worker concentrates on the core issue, making the decision to take a business trip next week or to stay with Peter. Generally, the closest problem in time proximity needs to be taken care of first. However in this situation, the timing is simultaneous but the hierarchy of needs is debatable. On the one hand, Peter's needs would seem to outweigh the needs of the business trip. On the other hand, Mary's business trip is also important. As a result, the crisis worker also does not respond to all of the panic stricken irrationalizations Mary uses. Instead, the worker ignores those and concentrates on making a well thought out and ordered decision based on all of the facts at hand.

Protection

The crisis worker safeguards clients from engaging in harmful, destructive, detrimental, and unsafe feelings, behaviors, and thoughts that may be psychologically or physically injurious or lethal to themselves or others.

Unlike any other form of counseling or psychotherapy, safety is always a primary concern and indeed, has its own specific step in crisis intervention. Moral, ethical, and legal considerations make safety and the protection of clients, significant others, and the crisis worker paramount. Safety issues are constantly assessed from the beginning to the end of crisis intervention and apply across the board from minimal to severe impairment on all of the TAF scales.

Providing protection focuses on shielding and defending clients to the degree they are unable to do so for themselves. Although the strategy can be used to assist clients in the resolution of affective and cognitive reactions, providing protection has special application when clients' behavioral reactions pose a danger to self or others. Providing protection is probably most critical with clients whose reactions range from marked to severe on the severity scales of the TAF. Crisis workers must therefore be familiar with the process by which involuntary commitment (hospitalization without the client's permission or willingness to go) is done. Each state is different as to who can initiate this process and communities also differ with respect to the procedures to carry out the process. The guidelines about transporting dangerous clients also differ from state to state, and even county to county. We encourage you to obtain information about involuntary commitment procedures and the transporting of dangerous clients through local governmental offices.

At its minimum, protection occurs when the crisis worker shields vulnerable individuals from secondary victimization after a traumatic experience. Acting as advocate for a rape victim as she goes through interrogation and evidence gathering or being sure recently widowed elderly persons are not taken advantage of by unscrupulous business practices are protective features that are part of good crisis intervention. When clients become so severely impaired that they are suicidal or homicidal, it is up to the crisis worker to become proactive and either find support systems that will watch over the person while he or she is suicidal or homicidal, or inform authorities who will take the person into protective custody.

When homicidal ideation is present, the worker must notify intended victims. Based upon the Tarasoff (Tarasoff v. Board of Regents of the University of California, 1976) case the crisis worker must inform authorities or the intended victim if there is a clear and present danger and the intended victim is identified or otherwise known by the crisis worker unless legal statute dictates otherwise. The notion is that incarcerating the client keeps not only the intended victim, but the client safe as well and offers less harm than if nothing were said or done (Thompson, 1983).

MARY: (Vehement and heated) I am so pissed with my husband. You know what he said, he said he didn't care. Peter is a big boy he can stay in the hospital by himself. He said I was just babying him by staying with him. Why didn't I come home so we could have "alone" time. If I get a chance, I'll make sure he gets his alone time, permanently.

CW: If you are telling me you want to kill your husband, I won't let you do that. I want you to stay safe and him no matter how badly he treats you and no matter how badly you feel.

MARY: (Struggling for control). Kill him, no way. But I could fix it so that he would have no reason to want "alone" time again.

CW: I guess I didn't understand, what do you mean?

MARY: Are you dense? Take a knife and do a little surgery.

CW: I understand you are super angry right now. However, I cannot ethically allow that anger to get you or anybody else hurt. I think we need to get you away from him to cool down for awhile. I want you to get on the phone right now and call someone. How about your sister? If you don't, I will call the authorities.

MARY: You'd turn me in. You said whatever we said was private. What kind of counselor are you anyway?

CW: A counselor who is not going to let you go to jail, get hurt, or hurt someone else. I am sorry you feel I would betray you, but legally, ethically, and morally I can't permit that to happen. Will you pick up the phone or shall I?

MARY: (Starts sobbing) Alright I will do it. Just give me a minute. (Looks up)...I wouldn't do that. I might think of hurting him. We may not have the best relationship, but I wouldn't do that. He isn't a bad person. I'm just so scared for Peter right now.

CW: (Reaches over and touches Mary on the arm). Did I hear you right? You wouldn't do anything to your husband? Are you sure?

MARY: (Dries her tears) I'm sorry I scared you. Maybe I even scared me a little. But, no, I wouldn't hurt him not just because he is insensitive.

CW: Mary, I believe you. You don't strike me as a violent person. However, I need you to make a promise. If you ever think of doing anything to hurt him or anyone else or yourself, you call me. Will you do that?

MARY: Thanks for caring. Yes, I will do that. But don't worry. I couldn't hurt anyone.

At times, crisis work calls for courage on the part of the worker. The crisis worker stands his ground here and clearly and firmly tells Mary what the limits are and under her present emotional state he cannot just let her walk out of the office without some assurance that she has a safety net. Therefore, he determines to find her someone who she can have close physical and psychological contact with so she is not left alone to brood. There is no magic formula when a crisis of lethality is occurring. If Mary becomes agitated and threatening and will not respond to the worker, then safety measures need to be in place so that the worker can leave or, if Mary storms out of the building, then the worker must get in contact with the police department and warn them.

In this situation, Mary responded to the crisis. Notice the crisis worker did not simply take Mary's statement that she would not harm her husband at face value. Instead, he solicited a promise from her that she would call if she ever felt the need to carry out her threat. It may sound like the crisis worker is mothering or judging the client. However, because of what the client has been through, the crisis worker makes a judgment that Mary is very fragile emotionally. While it is right for her to be angry, she does not have the right to threaten another person.

Levels of Intervention

Because clients' reactions to crises vary in regard to intensity, the nine strategies previously discussed must be adapted to address these variations. Matching the level of intervention to the severity of reactions is critical for two reasons. First, to be effective, crisis workers must use the level of intervention appropriate for the level of severity. Not doing so results in clients believing they were not helped. For example, clients who need to be guided as they work to resolve a crisis will not feel supported if crisis workers are passive. On the other hand, clients who simply need someone to listen will be annoyed and frustrated if crisis workers insist on giving advice.

Second, significant clinical errors of not taking action to prevent clients from harming themselves or others may result if the incorrect intervention level is used. Negligence can be applied in these situations and may result in crisis workers being held legally liable for the death of the client or another person.

The levels of intervention fall into three broad categories: "indirect", "collaborative", and "direct". These are best seen as a continuum with "indirect" and "direct" forming the poles. Table 2.1 gives examples of typical responses for the three levels as they are used with different reactions. Table 2.2 is a description of this interface.

Table 2.1 Level of Intervention

LEVEL OF INTERVENTION

	INDIRECT	COLLABORATIVE	DIRECT
AFFECTIVE	You seem sad/angry/afraid.	Talking about your sadness/anger/fear together may not be so uncomfortable.	Tell me about your sadness/anger/fear.
BEHAVIORAL	What are you doing to resolve the crisis?	Let me help you figure out what needs to be done.	I want you to stop (or start) _____ right now.
COGNITIVE	Are there other ways to understand what has happened?	Let's come up with other ways to think about what happened.	I need you to concentrate on _____ right now.

Table 2.2 Interactions with Domains

Affective/Indirect – invites clients' to express affective reactions in a safe way.

Affective/Collaborative – enlists clients' alliance with crisis worker in exploration of affective reactions.

Affective/Direct – instructs clients to communicate affective reactions.

Behavioral/Indirect – requests clients' cooperation in discontinuing or initiating behavior that will hinders or supports resolution of crisis.

Behavioral/Collaborative – initiates partnership between clients and crisis worker to facilitate discontinuing or initiating behavior that hinders or supports resolution of crisis.

Behavioral/Direct – commands clients to discontinue or initiate behavior that hinders or supports resolution of crisis.

Cognitive/Indirect – asks clients to review interpretation of crisis.

Cognitive/Collaborative – begins affiliation between clients and crisis worker to examine the interpretation of crisis.

Cognitive/Direct – corrects and focuses clients' interpretation of crisis.

Matching the level of intervention is coupled with scores of the severity scales on the TAF. The more severe the reactions, the more direct the intervention that is needed. Scores for each severity scale as well as the total score are used to determine the level of intervention. Below we give guidelines for selecting the level of intervention best suited for an individual client.

Direct Intervention

Direct intervention is used when clients have at least one reaction assessed as "marked" to "severe" on the TAF or whose total severity score is above 22. The goal of this level of intervention is to protect clients from being taken advantage of in some way or harming themselves or others. Clients who need direct intervention are extremely vulnerable and generally unable to perform tasks needed for daily living. In fact, clients experiencing this level of reaction exacerbate the crisis by unregulated expression of feelings, making decisions that are not based in reality, and behaving in ways that are dangerous to self or others. Crisis workers function as a manager with these clients. Much of the time direct interventions will begin with "I" – "I [crisis worker] want/need you to …." This level of intervention *instructs* clients and to a degree promotes dependency on crisis workers. Care must be exercised, however, to prevent undue dependence.

Collaborative Intervention

Collaborative intervention is used when clients' reactions fall primarily into the "low" to "moderate" range of severity on the TAF with the total severity score being from 13 to 22. The goal of this intervention level is to work with clients in sorting through the crisis. Clients who benefit from this level of intervention are obviously in crisis and need considerable assistance to resolve the crisis. Generally speaking, the expression of feelings is controlled with effort, communication of thoughts is vague, and behaviors may be erratic but usually not dangerous to self or others. Collaborative interventions involve a "we" approach in which crisis workers *partner* with clients, helping clients to organize resources and activate coping-skills to resolve the crisis.

Indirect Intervention

Indirect intervention is used with clients whose reactions mostly fall into the "minimal" range on the TAF or whose total severity score ranges from 3 to 12. The goal for indirect intervention is to activate clients' coping mechanisms and problem solving skills. This level of intervention is helpful for clients who to some extent are at a loss as to where to begin in resolving the crisis. These clients are typically aware of and can express their feelings, struggle to organize and articulate their thoughts, and behave within socially acceptable norms. Crisis workers *listen* and act as a sounding board for this group of clients. Clients are capable of responding to inquiries and are able to generate solutions rather quickly. The pronoun "you" is used often in indirect interventions: "What are you feeling?", "Are there other ways you can think about the situation?", and "What can you do to resolve the situation?".

Reflection Questions

1. *What strategies are you most comfortable using? Explain your response.*

2. *What strategies are you most uncomfortable using? Explain your response.*

3. *Describe how you feel about each of the three levels of intervention. How will these change the way you talk with clients?*

References

Baldwin, B. A. (1979). Crisis intervention: An overview of theory and practice. *The Counseling Psychologist, 8,* 43–52.

Carlson, E. B. (1997). *Trauma assessment: A clinician's guide.* New York: Guilford Press.

Cohen, E. (1990). Confidentiality, counseling and clients who have AIDS: Ethical foundations of a modern rule. *Journal of Counseling and Development, 66,* 282-286.

Dryden, W. (1984). *Rational-emotive therapy: Fundamentals and innovations.* London: Croom Helm.

James, R. K., & Gilliland, B. E. (2001). *Crisis intervention strategies* (5ᵗʰ ed.). Monterey, CA: Brooks/Cole.

Ellis, A. (1973). *Humanistic psychology: The rational-emotive approach* .New York: Julian.

Ellis, A. (1984). Foreword. In W. Dryden, *Rational-emotive therapy: Fundamentals and innovations.* (pp. i-xv). London: Croom Helm.

Hobbs, M. (1984). Crisis intervention in theory and practice: A selective review. *The British Psychological Society, 5,* 21–34.

Kleespies, P. M., Deleppo, J. D., Mori, D. L., & Niles, B. L. (1998). The emergency interview. In P. M. Kleespies (Ed.), *Emergencies in mental health practices: Evaluation and management* (pp. 41–74). New York: Guilford Press.

Lindemann, E. (1944). Symptomatology and management of acute grief. *American Journal of Psychiatry, 101,* 141–148.

Lindemann, E. (1956). The meaning of crisis in individual and family. *Teachers College Record, 57,* 310.

Matsakis, A. (1992). *I can't get over it: A handbook for trauma survivors.* Oakland, CA: New Harbinger Publications.

McFarlane, A. C., & Yehuda, R. (1996). Resilience, vulnerability, and course of posttraumatic reactions. In B. A. van der Kolk, A. C. McFarlane, & L. Weissaeth (Eds.), *Traumatic Stress* (pp. 155–181). New York: Guildford Press.

Miller, K., & Iscoe, I. (1963).The concept of crisis: Current status and mental health implications. *Human Organizations, 22,* 195–201.

Myer, R. A. (2001) *Assessment for crisis intervention: A three dimensional model.* Monterey, CA: Brooks/Cole.

Naugle, A. E., & Follette, W. C. (1998). A functional analysis of trauma symptoms. V. M. Follette, J. I. Ruzek, & F. R. Abueg (Eds.), *Cognitive-behavioral therapies for trauma* (pp. 48–73). New York: Guilford Press.

Novaco, R. W., & Chemtob, C. M. (1998). Anger and trauma. In V. M. Follette, J. I. Ruzek, & F. R. Abueg (Eds.), *Cognitive-behavioral therapies for trauma* (pp. 162–190). New York: Guilford Press.

Shalev, A. Y. (1996). Stress versus traumatic stress: From acute homeostatic reactions to chronic psychopathology. In B. A. van der Kolk, A. C. McFarlane, & L. Weisaeth (Eds.), *Traumatic Stress: The effects of overwhelming experience on mind, body, and society* (pp. 77–101). New York: Guilford Press.

Stuhlmiller, C., & Dunning, C. (2000). Challenging the mainstream: From pathogenic to salutogenic models of posttrauma intervention. In J. M. Violanti, D. Paton, & C. Dunning (Eds.), *Posttraumatic stress intervention: Challenges, issues, and perspectives* (pp.10-42). Springfield, IL: Charles C. Thomas Publisher.

Sue, D. W., & Sue, D. (1999). *Counseling the culturally different: Theory and practice,* (2nd ed.). New York: John Wiley and Sons.

Tarasoff v. Board of Regents of the University of California, 551 P.2d334 (19765).

Thompson, A. (1983). *Ethical concerns in psychotherapy and their legal ramification.* Lanham, MD: University Press of America.

Valent, P. (1998). *Trauma and fulfillment therapy.* Philadelphia: Brunner/Mazel.

van der Kolk, B. A. (1996a). Trauma and memory. In B. A. van der Kolk, A. C. McFarlane, & L. Weisaeth (Eds.), *Traumatic Stress: The effects of overwhelming experience on mind, body, and society* (pp. 279-302). New York: Guilford Press.

van der Kolk, B. A. (1996b). The body keeps score: Approaches to the psychobiology of posttraumatic stress disorder. In B. A. van der Kolk, A. C. McFarlane, & L. Weisaeth (Eds.), *Traumatic Stress: The effects of overwhelming experience on mind, body, and society* (pp. 214–241). New York: Guilford Press.

van der Veer, G. (1998). *Counselling and therapy with refugees and victims of trauma* (2nd ed.). New York: John Wiley and Sons.

Violanti, J. M. (2000). Scripting trauma: The impact of pathogenic intervention. In J. M. Violanti, D. Paton, & C. Dunning, (Eds.), *Posttraumaatic stress intervention: Challenges, issues, and perspective* (pp. 153–165). Springfield, IL: Charles Thomas Publisher.

Wagner, A. W., & Linehan, M. M. (1998). Dissociative behavior. In V. M. Follette, J. I. Ruzek, & F. R. Abueg (Eds.). *Cognitive-behavioral therapies for trauma,* pp. 191–225. New York: Guilford Press.

Worden, J. W., (1991). *Grief counseling and grief therapy: A handbook for the metal health practitioner* (2nd ed.). New York: Springer.

SECTION THREE

Integration Six Step Model with Strategies

Sections One and Two introduced you to all the elements needed to do crisis intervention including the Gilliland and James systematic model, rules of the road, basic counseling skills, crisis intervention strategies, and levels of intervention. This section puts all of these components of basic crisis intervention together. We will use the case of Mary that you were introduced to in Section Two as an example. We follow Mary through the intervention process. Learning activities and practice exercises are found on the CD-ROM.

Crisis Intervention with Mary

Section Two introduced you to Mary, a married white female whose 7 year old son, Peter, was recently diagnosed with leukemia. As you know, Mary works for a communications corporation, a job she landed within the past year. She works hard and enjoys the travel required by the position. Mary finds a sense of fulfillment in her job and feels appreciated by her co-workers. Mary's relationship with her husband has become increasingly strained since she began work at her current position. Although not openly hostile, the relationship is distant. The following is a condensed version of the crisis intervention process with Mary that took place immediately following Peter's diagnosis and during the initial treatment for his leukemia.

The crisis worker approaches working with Mary as if the situation is a crisis. As we discussed in Section One a defining characteristic of a crisis is the sense of disequilibrium being experienced by the client. Mary definitely is feeling this sense of disequilibrium. She is off balance in a least three areas of her life: (a) her concern and fear for Peter; (b) her career and being away on an upcoming business trip; and (c) the relationship she has with her husband. During the several days the crisis worker met with Mary the situation worsens and she begins to spiral out of control. Subsequently, the crisis becomes an emergency. Mary is horrified at the side effects of the treatments and intent on not wanting Peter to suffer any discomfort. The following excerpts focus on this issue.

Step 1. Defining the Problem.

Here, in Step 1, the crisis worker is attempting to focus on the most potent emergent feelings and concerns of Mary. While the crisis worker may see Mary over the course of Peter's treatment, the presenting problems that Mary brings to counseling will mean that the counselor will operate in a crisis mode. Therapy will focus specifically on problems the client is now having and seek to restore her to pre-crisis equilibrium if possible, even though it immediately seems clear that Mary's problems may be much more deep rooted. Emphasis will be placed on Mary's immediate needs as these unfold during the first few days of Peter's treatment. Although Mary's presenting problem is complex, the crisis worker is empathic, nonjudgmental, non-intrusive, supportive, and understanding of the many conflicted dynamics that are at work within the client.

The crisis worker exerts a great deal of patience with Mary who is, at times, so out of control that it is extremely difficult to get a handle on the problem. Paradoxically, while crisis intervention is time limited and time is of the essence, the crisis worker must take the time to adequately explore the problem as thoroughly as possible. One of our favorite statements when we deal with agitated clients is to repeat over and over, "We have plenty of time. Just take a deep breath for me, if you would, and let if out slowly. We really do have plenty of time to work on this."

> *Crisis Worker (CW)* 1.1: Right now you've got a real rat's nest of feelings. It sounds like it's mostly made out of glass, metal shards, and thorns too.

MARY 1.1: (Agitated and talking fast and in a high pitched voice pacing around the room as she talks). No shit Einstein. Why in the hell did the doctors want me to talk to you? Can you cure my son? No! NO one can, he is going to die. I can fell it in my bones. And that lousy husband of mine couldn't even come to the hospital. He said his work is too important, (lowers voice) as if mine isn't...So you're a shrink right? You're suppose to make me feel better. Make me feel better. Have you got kids? I want to talk with that doctor...and right now.

CW 1.2: Those are a lot of questions for me to answer. First, I want you to know how sorry I am this is happening, no one should have to watch their child face what Peter is facing. Help me to get this straight. You were referred to me to see if I can help you get some support and understand what is happening with your son. Sounds like this whole situation is so unbelievable to you that you barely can control the flood of emotions and you need someone to help you figure out what is happening.

MARY 1.2: (Highly agitated and now menacingly moves toward the crisis worker; slams a chair up against the wall). Sorry! SORRY! How in the hell do you have any comprehension what sorry is. You are the sorry son-of-a-bitch. Now I want to see the Goddamn doctor and see him now and not be shoved off on some shrink like I am crazy. By God! I can show you how crazy I can be. (Slams the chair against the wall again)

CW 1.3: (Stands up and keeps distance between the client and himself with an open stance ready to leave the room or defend himself. Opens space up between himself and the client). No! I don't know what it is like to be in the awful place you are in right now, but I can sure see the tremendous stress, fear, and anxiety you are under right now and I can feel sorry for you or anyone in that terrible pressure cooker with all the decisions you have to make, and I will take as much time as necessary to help you get some control back in your life. I wonder if you could just at least sit down and take one deep breath. Could you please do that?

MARY 1.3: (Stops her pacing, sits down, and takes a deep breath). You mean that? ...That you're sorry this is happening. I want to believe that. I just know I can't do this on my own. The doctors said that Peter will be alright, but that it won't be easy. His doctor wants to keep him in the hospital to do a couple more tests and begin treatment tomorrow or the next the day. I have to have help. I have a good job and, well, I really like what I do. I told them nothing is wrong, that I would be taking only the morning off. My team is counting on me.

CW 1.4: I appreciate you sitting down and getting a breath or two. I am not sure how I would handle all that. That's a tough place to be, being pulled in two directions. Wanting to stay with Peter and also not let the people at work down.

MARY 1.4: I know they can handle it but I still really like what I do. But I know Peter needs me. My mother died of cancer and...well I know how hard that was for her. This is reminding me of that.

CW 1.5: Now this seems like the same thing. Dredging up all those bad memories.

MARY 1.5: That was six years ago, but when I remember what she went through, it seems like just yesterday and now it starts all over again. I don't know if I can do this. I know I have to help Peter right now, he is the most important thing to me, but I just don't know if I can handle it. (Shoulders sag and starts sobbing uncontrollably).

The objective of this initial exploratory step is to teach the crisis worker what it most feels like to be Mary at this particular moment and what is most problematic for her right now. The crisis worker attempts to encapsulate and summary clarify both the content and the feelings of the client. By doing so, he attempts to find how she really does feel and think about the multiple dilemmas she is facing. The crisis worker learns that Mary is being pulled by her love and concern for Peter and her commitment to her career. He also discovered that Mary believes her husband is less than supportive of her and that her mother died a hard death from cancer. These issues merge into a tidal wave of raw emotions and convulsive thinking that washes over the situation. The crisis worker uses this initial session to facilitate as much self-discovery and autonomy as possible so that the client does not become dependent on the crisis worker. For neophyte counselors, this is a major task. Safety of the client is a concern but the same is true of the crisis worker. For a client in acute crisis it is all too tempting to attempt to intervene and fix everything. That course of action is fraught with peril and should be avoided as much as possible.

In the initial meetings with clients, the crisis worker is also concerned about safety. Mary's last statement raised red flags for the crisis worker and he immediately addresses these with Mary. Notice in this next stage the manner is which the crisis worker directly addresses his concerns about the safety of Mary, Peter, and her husband. For beginning counselors this process can be difficult. We recommend that if you have never asked a person this type of question you practice saying those words prior to seeing clients who are in crisis.

Step 2. Safety

Mary's affective reaction has shifted from being angry to that of overwhelming sadness.

CW 2.1: It is just overwhelming right now. (Reaches over and gently touches Mary's fore arm and remains quiet, but keeps physical touch lightly on Mary's fore arm while she grieves).

MARY 2.1: (Catches her breath). I don't know. I am tired. I couldn't sleep last night. The bed they [hospital] gave wasn't comfortable and I couldn't stop thinking about Peter and my mother.

CW 2.2: It must feel like you have been run over by a train.

MARY 2.2: (Looking down). A couple of trains would be more like it. I just can't get the picture of my mother out of my head. When I talked with my husband last night he wasn't very helpful. (Looks up). You know what he asked, why didn't I come home so we could have "alone" time…If I get a chance I'll make sure he gets his alone time, permanently. I could have killed him on the spot.

CW 2.3: Are you saying that you want to kill your husband? I won't let you do that. I want you to stay safe and him no matter how badly he treats you or Peter and no matter how badly you feel.

MARY 2.3: (Shrugs her shoulder). Kill him, no, no way. At least not him anyway.

CW 2.4: I guess I didn't understand, what do you mean?

MARY 2.4: No, I wouldn't kill him…I just keep thinking of my mother and watching her waste away. I just can't let that happen to Peter.

CW 2.5: I don't understand. What do you mean?

MARY 2.5: I just can't let him waste away like my mother did. The treatments almost killed her. I don't want that to happen to Peter…(Looks up and makes eye contact). You know Peter has always wanted to go to Disney World. I was thinking about taking him after he gets out of the hospital.

CW 2.6: Disney World sounds nice. Have you talked with the doctors about that?

MARY 2.6: Not yet, but it doesn't make any difference. I want Peter to have fun. I won't let him suffer.

CW 2.7: I'd want my son to have fun also. But you said something that concerns me. What do you mean you won't let Peter suffer?

The crisis worker is beginning to sense that something is amiss with Mary. Although she is understandably tired, her statements indicate something more ominous underlies Disney World. Mary is also identifying Peter's situation with that of her mother. This perception concerns the crisis worker as Mary states several times that she cannot allow Peter in her words to waste away. Coupled with the mention of her wanting to kill her husband, the crisis worker begins moving in the direction of viewing the situation as being an emergency.

MARY 2.7: I mean I want him to have fun and be happy. He doesn't look sick and I don't want the treatments to make him sick. (Looks down). But when he does get sick I know what I have to do.

CW 2.8: Mary, what is it you have to do?

MARY 2.8: (Starts sobbing) I can't let him suffer...I won't let him suffer.

CW 2.9: (Gently squeezes Mary on the arm). Mary, are you thinking of killing Peter?

MARY 2.9: (Continues crying)...yes I guess I am. But killing him, just not letting him suffer. But not just him, I couldn't go on either.

CW 2.10: You are thinking of killing him and yourself?

MARY 2.10: You won't tell anyone, will you?

CW 2.11: Mary, I have to tell someone if you are serious. I can't let you murder your son and then commit suicide.

MARY 2.11: (Looks stunned and makes eye contact). Not murder, I won't let him suffer.

CW 2.13: Have you thought of when and how you are going to do this?

MARY 2.12: No. It just came to me last night. First I want to take him to Disney World and well it wouldn't be for a long time.

CW 2.13: Mary, am I hearing you correctly, you don't have a plan or a time?

MARY 2.13: (Cries uncontrollably). I must be awful for thinking about that. I just keep seeing my mother and I don't want Peter to look like her.

CW 2.14: You really love him and I don't blame you for not wanting the same to happen to him as your mother. It is much too early to know what is going to happen. You said yesterday the doctors said he will be fine. I want you to focus on that. Can you do that?

MARY 2.14: (Dries her tears). I d-don't know. Maybe. I want to, but my mother...suffering... wanting to die...at the last...but couldn't, so much pain. Yes, I think I can. I don't know. I want to but I don't know.

CW 2.15: I can't be your husband, but I will do all I can to help you through this and that includes talking to your husband or anybody else to get you some support. But I am concerned about your thinking that killing your son and yourself will solve this. It will not. I will want a written statement that you will not kill yourself or your son before you leave here. If I am not fully convinced, I will not let you leave the hospital.

MARY 2.15: That's terrible! How could you turn me in? All I want is some relief and no pain for my son.

CW 2.16: I understand you think I am not being helpful, but I am ethically and morally bound not to let my clients get hurt, hurt themselves or hurt others. I hope you understand that and can do what I have asked, but if you can't I will do what I have said. A no harm contract means that if you have even the slightest thought about carrying through on any of those thoughts you will call me and contact me or come to the hospital and admit yourself. What do you wish to do?

MARY 2.16: I know you're only doing what you think is best. But it is just so hard to think him suffering and I can't do anything about it.

When dealing with safety concerns, the crisis worker does not mince words. Very directive and clear closed-end questions are given to Mary to determine the intensity and degree of the threat. Mary's thoughts of her mother dying are overriding her judgment and spilling into the current situation. The crisis worker ignores Mary's grief for her mother, instead focusing on the threat of her killing Peter and herself. He is operating in real time, and the only thing that really counts in crisis work is what is happening here-and-now. Although Mary seems to be composed at the moment, the crisis worker has real concerns about her lethality. The absence of any defined plan or method or time diminishes the threat somewhat, but does not mean she is non-lethal given her current emotional and cognitive state. He lets Mary know this and asks her to call him or come to the hospital if she has these thoughts again. While it may seem ludicrous to take a client's word on such a serious matter, very few clients will go back on their word once it is given. However, in the final equation, the crisis worker will rely on the Triage Assessment Scale assessment to determine what he will do with Mary.

Using the Triage Assessment Form (TAF) to make an estimate of the client's current lethality level, he judges that Mary's affect is at a 7 due to its liability and effort is required to control her emotions as she absorbs the meaning of Peter's illness in her life. It is difficult to assess Mary's mood in this short period but it does seem to be more negative with little hope or optimism. The crisis worker rates her as a 9 on the cognitive dimension because of the intrusive thoughts of the event that are barely within her control. She is overwhelmed and experiencing disequilibrium. Her problem solving and decision-making are being adversely affected by obsessiveness, self-doubt, and confusion both in regard to others and her own self-image. Her self-talk is negative about the situation and her perception of it is noticeably different than the reality of the situation warrants. Peter's condition is serious, but according to the doctors not life threatening unless he gets no treatment. Her behavioral rating is a 7. Although she is immobile, unable to cope very well at this time, Mary may become energized, and seek to solve her problem by killing her child and herself. Her total TAF score is a 23 which puts her on the high end of the "moderately impaired" range. The crisis worker's assessment means that he will have to be vigilant with Mary in order to identify changes that might suggest she is losing the ability to control her impulse to kill Peter and herself. Any increase in this score would mean immediately placing Mary in a supervised environment where she could not hurt herself or others. In that regard, constant assessment is critical and must be done on a moment-to-moment basis. In regard to her homicidal ideation, a missing ingredient is a well-defined plan. While Mary may have the motivation and the means, she has not formulated a plan to carry out either act. That diminishes her potential lethality a great deal.

CW 2.17: I believe what you are saying, but I am concerned about you getting so overwhelmed that you might start thinking more seriously about killing Peter and yourself. You are under tremendous pressure and I want to make sure that we work together so that you can begin to feel some relief. I believe this is not unsolvable and that we can work through the sadness and scared feelings you are having. But to make sure we have the opportunity I want to make sure that you don't do something you regret. So I want to enter into a no harm contract with you whereby you consent not to do anything to harm others or yourself for that matter so that we can have the time that we need to get things back on an even keel. I need your agreement on that and for you to sign it. Can you do that for me?

MARY 2.17: (Somewhat suspiciously). I guess...I don't know! That sounds kind of weird. How long and what do I have to agree to?

CW 2.18: I'd like to put this in place for a week and have the option of renewing it thereafter. You'd simply agree not to hurt yourself or others. If you start having those kinds of thoughts, you'd agree to call me or the hotline at the hospital. You must do that, busy signals or I'm not in don't count. You must get through no matter what time of the day or night.

MARY 2.18: I guess...for a week but it still sounds weird. You'd trust me to keep my word?

CW 2.19: Is there any reason I shouldn't? I believe what the doctors say. I believe Peter can get better. You need to believe that for right now and put that billboard right smack in front of you. Like a heads up display every time those unbidden thoughts about your mother start to pop up. Can you do this? I will be with you every step of the way. We will get more support in this so it doesn't seem like you are carrying the world on your shoulders all alone. Do you trust me to stay with you and help you through this crisis? Can you commit to it?

MARY 2.19: No, I'll keep my word. It is good. I'll do it.

The crisis worker uses a number of owning statements about his present concern for the client and does so in a clear, clean manner that leaves nothing to the imagination. The contract will read the same way. Figure 3.1 is a sample living contract that can be used with clients who are threatening some type of harm to themselves or others. In this situation, the crisis worker uses a "living contract" to help stabilize her for a short period of time. For most clients, signing a living contract is a moral agreement to do something that psychologically takes on the weight of a legal agreement. He is also providing support and encouragement for Mary without making false promises he may not be able to keep. Unlike other forms of counseling that might view such support as dependency creating, the crisis worker is concerned about immediately giving the client hope and will bargain for time to get the client back into homeostasis.

Figure 3.1 Living Contract

I _____ agree not to harm myself for the next week. I promise to call
      (client name)

_____ if my suicidal thoughts and feelings become too strong to control.
      (crisis worker name)

If I cannot contact my crisis worker I will call the Crisis Hotline at _____.
                                          (phone number)

_____ _____   _____
(client name)   (date)   (crisis worker name)

Step 3. Providing Support

It is very important for the crisis worker to be supportive of Mary through both verbal and nonverbal communications. Supportive words and behaviors must be clear, empathic, genuine, and connote positive and unconditional regard for the client. The crisis worker is not being redundant when he says these supportive statements over again. Mary clearly needs to hear these words come through the emotional tidal wave that is currently submerging her.

> *CW 3.1:* I know you had reservations about talking to me after getting the news about Peter having leukemia and the doctor not seeming to want to answer your questions. I also would guess that it's doubly hard to talk to a person you don't know about everything that is going on. I want you to know I appreciate the opportunity to help you through figuring out what is best for Peter's treatment and you. That may sound awfully trite but I want you to know we're clearly in this together and that we'll see it through together. I have faith that you will get through this and will work very hard with you to see that happens.

> *MARY 3.1:* Thanks for helping. I do feel all alone. I just don't know what to do.

The crisis worker's statements are not a sales pitch. He says these things to provide an anchor for a client who is adrift at the moment and feels very little support from others. Mary needs a safe harbor to rest in for awhile and the crisis worker will endeavor to provide it. The crisis worker also seeks to find out what other environmental supports are available for Mary.

> *CW 3.2:* I am wondering if there is anyone you could talk to and get some support from?

> *MARY 3.2:* Not really. Maybe my sister, but she works too. I don't know. I guess I need to call the church, but we don't go that often. I don't even know my neighbors that well.

> *CW 3.3:* Of the church members, neighbors or family who right now would be best?

> *MARY 3.3:* (Big Sigh). Well, I can call my sister. We used to be close until I got married. She doesn't like my husband. We only get together on holidays...sometimes. She really knows me and has always been there for me in the past.

> *CW 3.4:* I think it is a good idea to call her. You said you used to be close. This isn't about your marriage. It is about you and Peter right? Let's think about what you need to say to her and how you can keep this on track about helping Peter and not turning it into a bitch session about your husband.

> *MARY 3.4:* Thanks, I mean I know what I would say, but she always bitches at me about my husband. I guess after some of the things I have been thinking it would be a good idea to have someone to talk to, but it is kind of humbling and embarrassing.

> *CW 3.5:* I tell you what, let's practice. You be your sister and I'll be you. Maybe that way we can figure this out so it doesn't turn into an awesome task.

Mary is reluctant to contact her sister yet seems to want to ask her for support. The crisis worker senses this ambivalence and joins with her to practice approaching her sister. Situations such as this are common for a person in crisis. The strain of the situation can leave the person unable to think through simple tasks. In this situation, Mary is so overwhelmed by Peter's diagnosis she is uncertain how to approach her sister. The crisis worker offers to role play this with her in order to help Mary get some ideas of things she would want to say and how to say these when she contacts her sister.

MARY 3.5: Do you know of anyplace that I can get some more information about all this?

CW 3.6: I'm glad you asked. I was going to tell you anyway. The "Caring Place" is an agency that has support groups for parents whose children have cancer.

MARY 3.6: Cancer, I can't stand the sound of that word.

CW 3.7: That is tough to hear, but it is only a word, a word that you can get control over. The "Caring Place" has groups several times a week plus they have a lot of information and they are certainly about getting control over that dreaded word.

MARY 3.7: I don't know. I have to think about it. I'm not sure I'm ready for that. Spilling my guts in front of strangers.

CW 3.8: That is one option. You might try the American Cancer Society. They are more informational than support group oriented. They even have a web site. As a matter of fact, I have a list of web sites that might be helpful.

MARY 3.8: Thanks. Maybe that wouldn't be too bad an idea, looking at the web sites. I feel so dumb, why didn't I think of that?

The crisis worker may have to provide direct information to clients who are unaware of some of the options they may have. While looking to past support persons is helpful, clients may not have the vaguest notion about what kinds of societal support systems are available to them. At such times, the crisis worker provides that information and will offer to act as a go-between if clients are unable or reticent about doing it themselves.

Step 4. Examining Alternatives

Even though there may be emotional supports and coping mechanisms available such as Mary's sister, many times clients are so immobilized that they may have concluded that they have few or no viable options left. Thus, crisis work may be viewed as a moving point on a continuum line from being nondirective to very directive in assisting clients. The client may be judged to move back and forth on this line. To that extent, if the client is immobile, the crisis worker will be directive. If the client is completely mobile, the crisis worker will be nondirective. If the client is partially mobile as in the case of Mary, the crisis worker will be collaborative.

The session continues as the crisis worker attempts to help Mary get a clearer understanding of Peter's illness and the impact that has on her life. The goal is for Mary to activate coping mechanisms that she has used in the past. However, the crisis worker must continue to help Mary focus as she waivers between being immobile, avoiding the crisis, and at times, approaching it in a constructive manner.

CW 4.1: Mary, I'd like you to think of some other coping behaviors that have got you by tough times when you were either angry at others or depressed about the way things were going and couldn't seem to get it together.

MARY 4.1: Well, I used to work out a lot. Going to the gym always relieved my stress, and even helped me think better. There were three or four of us who met four times a week. Since getting the new job I just don't seem to have the time right now.

CW 4.2: Maybe you couldn't be with them, but what's to keep you from getting back into a training program for yourself?

52

MARY 4.2: I don't know. I just kinda lost interest since starting the new job. Now with everything…(starts crying again).

CW 4.3: The sadness and the terror don't go away easily, and getting a workout in won't magically get rid of those, but part of taking care of Peter is taking care of yourself. I wonder if you could just do a little everyday, sorta working you way back into a full training regimen. What would be a small start?

MARY 4.3: Well, maybe I could find some time to start working out again. I just don't know, I can't leave Peter, he is so helpless. If you could have seen him when they put in the needle for the chemo today.

CW 4.4: I have an idea. I think you could get a work out in here at the hospital's staff fitness facility. They let other out-of-town relatives use it, so I don't see why you couldn't. There is a gym connected with the hospital for the employees. But family members of patients can also use it for a small fee, I think it is $3 a day.

MARY 4.4: (Chuckles) Maybe Peter would like to see his mom start looking like one of Charlie's Angels…not that I ever did.

CW 4.5: I believe we could arrange for Peter to come and watch you work out. How about it? Want me to put that in motion?

MARY 4.5: Yes, I would like that. I guess it would be okay.

CW 4.6: I am glad to hear that…but you sound like you feel a little guilty about taking care of yourself.

MARY 4.6: What makes you say that…(silence). Okay you're right. I'm not sure so I don't know if I should leave him even to get something to eat. I wish I had some help. That husband of mine isn't.

CW 4.7: Do you want to ask him to come in and talk? Remember we have role played talking with your sister. Perhaps that isn't enough support.

MARY 4.7: You're right. I do need support and Peter does need his father. Would you talk with us together?

CW 4.8: I would be happy to. When do you think we can get together?

When examining alternatives in a crisis situation, social supports, behavioral coping mechanisms, and changing negative self-talk and irrational beliefs about the situation are all critical. The crisis worker is very directive in pointing out these areas to Mary and provides her with education and guidance as to how these affect her response to the situation and what the client can do about it. Many times a minor adjustment, such as pointing out conversations from previous sessions is all that is necessary to reintroduce behavioral coping mechanisms back into a client's life. At other times, entirely new resources or behaviors may have to be found, particularly if the client is no longer physically or mentally able to engage in former activities.

When we deal with the negative messages that are invariably highly irrational and have some catastrophic meaning attached to them when clients are going through a crisis, it is incumbent on the crisis worker to educate clients as to what they are doing cognitively to themselves. Such educative functions mean the crisis worker lays out the client's irrational belief system, disputes the "crazy" thinking, and helps the client put new positive, self-enhancing coping statements into operation. When doing so, the crisis worker focuses on one element of the problem at a time. While there may be many issues in regard to Mary's ability to be a good parent, the crisis worker understands Mary's self-concept is more than just that. By having this understanding, the crisis worker does not dismiss or discount the other issues facing Mary, such as the relationship with her husband and the death of her mother. Certainly these issues may be dealt with later in long-term therapy. Right now, the major flash point seems to be Mary's needs to take care of herself. Thus, this problem assumes first and highest priority in getting her back into a pre-crisis state of equilibrium and homeostasis.

Step 5. Making Plans

If alternatives have been examined thoroughly, then making plans will flow logically from Step 4 into concrete action steps. In Step 5, it is vital that Mary both understand and own the plan. A crisis worker instituted plan, no matter how elegant, which is forced on the client will most generally mean that Mary is either unwilling or unlikely to do something about it.

> *CW 5.1:* Considering what we have gone over, what do you think you major goal right now is and what can you do?

> *MARY 5.1:* Like we said, I need to talk with the doctor, but not by myself. I can call my sister to see when she can come down either later today or tomorrow. I need to take the paper with my questions with me so I can have my sister write down what the doctor says. I know he has told me Peter will be fine next week… but I still can't shake the feeling of abandoning Peter. What if something happens while I am talking with the doctor?

> *CW 5.2:* I know you are scared. We can talk with the nurses and ask them to check on him while you are gone. Who else were you going to contact?

> *MARY 5.2:* (Smiles). I was getting to it. I need to call work to let them know what is happening and also contact my church once I talk with the doctor.

> *CW 5.3:* Great. I'd like to see you tomorrow to see how things turn out. If you like I can even talk with you and Peter at the same time.

> *MARY 5.3:* Yes, I mean I don't know. I trust you. But I am not sure I can talk with you and Peter at the same time. I just don't know if I could keep from crying. He does seem to be doing good. You know what he told me today, "Don't worry Mom, I am doing fine. You don't have to treat me like a baby."

> *CW 5.4:* Good! Tomorrow we'll talk a good deal more about Peter and abandoning him and what that's all about.

While the client does not agree to all of what has been proposed it is a start. Throughout the course of the session the crisis worker has been continuously assessing the client on the TAF scale. While the client is a long way from being able to fully understand her misgivings about being away from Peter at this time, her verbal and nonverbal demeanor suggests she is more comfortable than she admits. Mary's ability to talk about her feelings and start planning what she will do diminish her affective and behavioral ratings. Her thinking is pretty much linear and logical and she has worked somewhat collaboratively with the counselor to come up with a plan. Yet, the sense of self doubt persists with respect to abandoning Peter suggesting her cognitive reaction is 5 and possibly a 6. Behaviorally the threat of Mary killing Peter and committing suicide seems distant; therefore, the crisis worker assesses the severity of her behavioral reaction as 5. Mary's affective reaction is assessed as a 5 at this time making the total TAF score a 15 or 16. This score suggests that a collaborative approach will be most effective with Mary as she continues to sort through the meaning of Peter's illness for her life.

Step 6. Obtaining Commitment.

Step 6 constitutes the commitment phase that is of vital importance in demonstrating the client's understanding and resolve to carrying out the plan. As planned, the next day the crisis worker meets with Mary after she and her sister talked with the doctor. They discuss the action steps but this time start with talking about what the doctor has said about Peter's condition. The crisis worker is interested in Mary taking care of herself and getting the support that she needs. Yet, he is sensitive to Mary's feelings that she needs to be with Peter and willing to move back to an earlier step in the systematic model if needed. He knows Mary' tension will not be resolved at this time and that he doesn't have to solve all the problems that make up her total crisis in one fell swoop. Nor does the crisis worker feel the need to affect an immediate "fix" of all the ills that assail Mary. It is the incremental move toward positive action that the client makes that is important. Before Mary leaves the session, she will have plans well in mind to make use of the options that have a good chance of succeeding. To that end, the crisis worker carefully goes over what is planned and gains a commitment from Mary to put her action steps into operation. To gain a clear commitment to action, we advocate that the client be given the chance to verbally summarize what is going to happen. In some situations a written agreement may be needed, but at the very least, the spoken intention of the client is an important symbol of commitment to action. If there are any missed points the crisis worker can go back over them.

> *CW 6.1:* So, could you now summarize for me what we are going to do?

> *MARY 6.1:* Well, I'm going to call the church and see if anyone can help me and contact the people at work to let them know what is going on and that I can't make the trip next week. I think that's all.

> *CW 6.2:* Good but remember we talked about two other things, one from yesterday and the other the day before.

> *MARY 6.2:* Okay, seeing about using the workout facilities at the hospital to workout, and…

> *CW 6.3:* Remember, if you start to feel like things are so bad you want to hurt your husband or yourself or Peter for that matter, you will call me no matter what. But if you can't get me what will you do?

> *MARY 6.3:* OK, I hadn't forgotten about that, don't worry. But I'll promise to call you if things get bad. I'll make an appointment with the secretary for us to get together tomorrow morning. How's that? And I will go to the hospital and check myself in if I start really feeling bad.

> *CW 6.4:* Good, want to shake on that.

> *MARY 6.4:* Sure, OK. (Shakes the crisis worker's hand)

This case illustrates the crisis intervention process with a complex situation. The crisis worker talks with Mary six times during Peter's first hospitalization to treat his leukemia. The sessions varied from 15 minutes to more than an hour, especially when the crisis worker was ensuring Mary's and Peter's safety. Mary is overwhelmed by the diagnosis of her son as having leukemia. As the crisis worker talks with Mary during the first few days after her son was hospitalized, he uncovers the crisis is complicated by the satisfaction she gets from work and the poor relationship she has with her husband. Together these issues result in Mary being confused with respect to her feeling and values. The crisis worker helps her begin the process of sorting through these concerns in an empathic, non-judgmental manner guiding Mary in the decision making process. To a limited degree, the crisis worker fosters some dependence on himself as he collaborates with her to resolve the dilemmas she faces. Throughout the process the crisis worker worked with Mary, the focus remained on the current situation. Staying focused on the current situation is critical for the resolution of the crisis.

Reflection Questions

1. What, if any issues in the case of Mary caused you concern? What about those issues was troubling?

2. Describe how the Crisis Workers addressed the issues that were a problem for you?

3. How would you address those or similar issues with clients?

SECTION FOUR

Case Studies for CD-ROM

The two scenarios presented in this section allow you to see crisis workers working with clients. Ethical guidelines on confidentiality and providing treatment prevent us from using actual clients. To do so would be intrusive and exploit the vulnerability of the clients. The reactions of the clients in the scenarios are based on our experience with numerous clients we have seen in our 40 years of combined experience. As is typical in crisis counseling, the crisis workers' knowledge of the client was limited prior to the session. The crisis workers were asked to provide assistance for a problem that was occurring at that time. The comfort of having the information that regularly accompanies a first session was not available. Both crisis workers showed composure in calming the clients and used creativity to help activate problem skills.

You may want to follow the intervention process by reading the transcript in the workbook while watching the CD-ROM. The CD-ROM can be stopped at any point in order for you to go directly to the exercises. The exercises are designed to assist you in expanding your crisis intervention skills. You can use these to identify the crisis workers' responses, test your competency at mapping responses, or to create and map alternative responses. Included in the exercises are questions to help you assess the clients' reactions in order to focus on the intervention process.

Please note that the entire session with the clients is not presented. Technical restrictions with respect to the limit of the CD-ROM make using the entire session impossible. We have selected the segments of the session that represent each of the six steps in the model described in Section One of the workbook. Also, be aware that colorful language is used by one of clients. This situation is not unusual when helping clients who are in crisis. We apologize if this offends anyone. However, we wanted the scenarios to be as realistic as possible.

CASE ONE: The Distraught Mother

This scenario takes place in a hospital. The situation involves a mother, Katherine, who rushed to the hospital after being told of a bus accident involving her 10 year-old son. The accident occurred while on a school field trip. Katherine only knows that many children received injuries, some injuries being potentially life threatening. She has been at the hospital for over 30 minutes and has received no information regarding the condition of her son. In fact, she is not even sure he was admitted to that specific hospital. One person has already attempted to talk to Katherine with no success. As you will see, this person only caused Katherine's crisis to intensify. Note that throughout the sessions the crisis worker, Dick, remains calm. Observe his tone of voice and the patience he uses to calm Katherine. This process is exceedingly important with clients who are angry. Crisis workers must be in control, not allowing the emotional reactions of clients to unsettle them. Katherine begins to relax as Dick shifts the focus of the session to helping Katherine put into place support systems she needs. The shift is critical if Katherine is to be of help to her son as he recovers from his injuries.

You may want to watch the video as you read the transcript or choose to simply read the transcript and watch the video separately. As you read through and watch the video we ask that you think about two things. First, what is the crisis for the client? Remember the same event can result in separate crises for different people. Understand it is the meaning a client assigns to an event that determines the crisis. Second, observe the client's affective, behavioral, and cognitive reactions to the crisis. How do these influence the crisis worker during the intervention process? You will find questions related to these two issues for each Step in the Systematic Model on the CD ROM, in addition to Response Mapping Exercises similar to those completed for Section Three.

Step 1: Defining the Problem

In this segment, Dick meets Katherine who is very angry about the manner in which the hospital staff has treated her. Not only is she angry about the treatment but also extremely anxious to find her son. The situation was made worse by a hospital employee who was not sensitive to her needs. Throughout the segment Dick must attend to Katherine's affective reactions regarding this incident, yet gather the information to determine if her son is in the hospital.

Notice Dick's approach in this segment and the way he handles Katherine's demands. Observe the way he acknowledges the validity of Katherine's insistence of finding her son while maintaining his position. If you are watching the CD ROM as you read the segment, pay attention to the way Dick uses his tone of voice to begin the process of calming Katherine.

Key: **Katherine = Mother**
              Dick = Psychologist

KATHERINE 1.1:	Great, god damn it! This hospital is . . . I have been waiting for like 30 minutes. Thirty fucking minutes for my child! And that moron that was just in here.
DICK 1.1:	Excuse me.
KATHERINE 1.2:	Oh great. Who the hell are you?
DICK 1.2:	I'm, I'm Dick James. I'm the psychologist here. I was asked to come down, I didn't get . . .
KATHERINE 1.3:	(interrupting) Oh, I've already, I've already talked to one of your psychologists. If you're anything like he is you might as well just get the fuck out of here.
DICK 1.3:	Okay. I understand, I understand that you are pretty upset right now and things haven't . . .
KATHERINE 1.4:	(interrupting) I want to know where my child . . . He called, he called my son, my son! He called my son "George". George. I told him nine times. My son's name is Jeremy. He's in a bus bus accident. (pause) Shit. And I know that there is a lot of other kids but for god's sake will you please find out what is going on with him?
DICK 1.4:	Okay, I've got Jeremy so, so far but I am sorry, I did not get your name.
KATHERINE 1.5:	Jeremy Smith. I am his mother, Katherine.
DICK 1.5:	Okay Katherine.
KATHERINE 1.6:	He is 10 years old. He's (pause) he's got red hair. He's the only one that in the class with red hair. Would you just go find him goddamn it? I don't even know if he is here. They told me one of three hospitals. They said,

"Most likely he is at this hospital". But if it's one like that one moron that was just in here, I'll never see my son again. Would you please go find my kid?

DICK 1.6:   Alright I am doing that as quickly as I possibly can. Okay?

KATHERINE 1.7:   Well, go, go!

DICK 1.7:   First of all though, there's just, I need to get, I need to get just a little bit of inform, information from you. And . . .

KATHERINE 1.8:   (interrupting) Oh, insurance! (pause) Is that what you want, is my fucking insurance?

DICK 1.8:   I'm not, I'm not concerned about insurance right, right now. I'm concerned. We have a lot of kids in here Katherine.

KATHERINE 1.9:   I don't care about the other kids. I mean, I care but I want to know about my kid! My kid!

DICK 1.9:   I understand.

KATHERINE 1.10:   My kid. I have been waiting longer than anybody else has here. Longer than anybody.

DICK 1.10:   That is what I want to do right now is I want to see if we can find your child. The child, the children have been sent to at least three hospitals, okay? And so, I want to be sure that we've, we've got Jeremy here. If we don't, then we'll find out where he is and we'll get you there.

KATHERINE 1.11:   Then why are you standing here?

DICK 1.11:   Because I wanna, I wanna get just a little bit of information from you, okay? Could you . . .

KATHERINE 1.12:   (interrupting) You have his name.

DICK 1.12:   I know.

KATHERINE 1.13:   You have my name.

DICK 1.13:   I know.

KATHERINE 1.14:   Bus accident. Shelby Elementary. Please, go find him. 10 years old. Red hair. God! What else? He's got a birthmark on his hip. What else do you wanna know?

DICK 1.14:   We're gonna need, we're gonna need to be able to do, to do some things. I wonder if you could just sit down. Okay? Would it be possible to do that?

KATHERINE 1.15:   No. I don't think that I can do that right now.

DICK 1.15:   Katherine, I really understand how angry you are and how con, how confusing and out of control things seem here, seem here. What I really want to do is to find all this out. I know, I know it's a mess. And we do have a mess here right now, okay? We've got, we've got over 40 kids that have come in, come in here. Uh, I know that it's really hard for you to understand. I know you've been waiting and frustrated.

KATHERINE 1.16:   Forty kids on the bus, they went to three different hospitals. For god's sakes!

DICK 1.16:   That's right.

KATHERINE 1.17:   Jesus, god. I mean. How tough is this?

DICK 1.17:   It's a really scary place to be Katherine. I mean, I, I can only imagine what it must be for you. What I want to do, is I want to go find out exactly whether we got your boy here or not. Uh, I am going to do that. I'd really like you to just to sit down though. And I don't mean to be difficult but can you just sit down for me, please? Would that be possible?

KATHERINE 1.18:   And he's my only child.

DICK 1.18:   I sure hear some fear in there.

KATHERINE 1.19:   I've had three miscarriages. Geez, I was old when I had him. For god sakes! He's my only . . . I live for this kid! And, and

DICK 1.19:   I get, I get that. And I am going to do the very best I can to get information to you. And, and let things just, if we can just calm down. I want to bring someone in here right now, okay?

KATHERINE 1.20:   (sigh)

DICK 1.20:   I know this is difficult for you. Can you tell me what grade he's in?

KATHERINE 1.21:   He's 10 years old.

DICK 1.21:   He's 10 years old. Would that be about the fifth, fifth grade?

KATHERINE 1.22:   Fifth grade, yes.

DICK 1.22:   Okay. Could you also, could you also give me his, uh homeroom, name? Do you, could you remember his homeroom teacher's name?

KATHERINE 1.23:   Yeah, yeah. Her name is, um, Pruitt! No, no, that was last year. Um . . .

DICK 1.23:   That's okay, you take your time.

KATHERINE 1.24:   Fuck. Um, Harris! Harris.

DICK 1.24:   Harris.

KATHERINE 1.25:	Yes.
DICK 1.25:	Mrs.? Ms.?
KATHERINE 1.26:	Does it really matter? It's a woman.
DICK 1.26:	Okay. Okay, fine. We'll . . . that's fine.
KATHERINE 1.27:	Just.
DICK 1.27:	Okay. That's the information I need. I'm going to have someone get it. As soon as I, as soon as I find out if we've got Jeremy here I'll be right back down and tell you. Okay?
KATHERINE 1.28:	It's been 35 minutes.
DICK 1.28:	I, I understand it's been, it's been awhile. But we are going to do this and moving as quickly as we possibly can.

Throughout this exchange, Dick balanced being empathic to Katherine's feelings and also moving forward to gather information needed to locate her son. With clients who are as angry as Katherine, crisis workers must be careful not to cause the client's anger to intensify, yet at the same time validate the feeling. Dick does well in this respect by remaining calm and repeatedly confirming the information Katherine has provided. This process helps her to express the anger while providing assurance that she is being taken seriously. As Dick calls Katherine by name throughout the segment, he also communicates that she is important, resulting in her beginning to become more composed. Finally, Dick does not allow himself to be sidetracked. Instead, he stays focused on Katherine and obtains the information he needs to locate her son.

Step 2: Safety

A few minutes have passed from the previous segment. In this segment, Dick recognizes that Katherine is bordering on hysteria and makes the decision to have someone stay with her while he is locating her son. Initially, Katherine is resistant to this idea, but eventually acquiesces. It is important to understand that in crisis situations safety issues extend beyond suicidal and homicidal ideations. Clients who are as emotionally charged as Katherine may behave irrationally, causing harm to themselves or others. Dick does not want to chance this situation happening with Katherine. Not leaving Katherine alone serves another purpose. Katherine has begun settling down and Dick wants this process to continue. He does not want to risk her becoming agitated again by being left alone. He also knows that having someone stay with her will communicate that the hospital is sensitive to her needs.

Notice Dick's patience throughout this segment. Rather than force Katherine to allow the psychological intern to stay, he convinces her it is a good idea. Observe that he does not allow Katherine's protest to deter him. Instead he uses owning statements to persuade her to allow the intern to stay.

Key: **Katherine = Mother**
Dick = Psychologist
Mimi = Psychology Intern

DICK 2.1:	I want to bring somebody in here right now, okay?

KATHERINE 2.1:	No, you don't have to do that.
DICK 2.2:	I, I know. And. But, it, this will help me and so I know that you're okay while I'm getting the information. I can do this quicker if you'll just, if you'll just let me do this, okay?
KATHERINE 2.2:	Okay, okay. Just hurry up it's, god, it's been 20 minutes or something.
DICK 2.3:	Okay. I'm, I'm I'm gonna go and find this out. I'm gonna have a young lady come in here and just sit with you for just a moment.
KATHERINE 2.3:	Okay. Okay. Just go find my kid.
DICK 2.4:	I'll be back just as quickly as I can. I know that this is frightening and terribly, terribly scary for you.
KATHERINE 2.4:	It is awful! He's my only child.
DICK 2.5:	I'm going to get the information for you, okay?
KATHERINE 2.5:	Okay.
DICK 2.6:	You just, you stick with me. I understand that you want action and that you are frustrated and you're scared. If you can do this, that will allow me to know that you're safe and that you're okay and that I can get this done. Okay.
KATHERINE 2.6:	Please, hurry.
DICK 2.7:	It seems slow but this is the best way to it, okay?
KATHERINE 2.7:	Please, hurry.
DICK 2.8:	I'm gonna get Mimi. Okay.
KATHERINE 2.8:	What's his name again? What's my kid's name again?
DICK 2.9:	It's Jeremy. It's Jeremy. Jeremy Smith. Okay.
KATHERINE 2.9:	Alright.
DICK 2.10:	Ms. Harris' class. Fifth grade. Shelby Elementary.
KATHERINE 2.10:	Yeah.
DICK 2.11:	Okay? I've got it. Okay Katherine, I'm gonna go. I'm gonna get uh, one of our interns in here. She's gonna sit with you awhile. This will allow me to find this out and be sure that you are still okay. Alright? Her name is Mimi Yablonsky and I am going to go get her right now, okay?
KATHERINE 2.11:	Just go, just go. Just hurry.

DICK 2.12:	Okay. Alright.

KATHERINE 2.12:	Please.

(Psychologist leaves and returns with the intern)

DICK 2.13:	Now, Mimi, uh, this is Katherine Smith. Katherine is the mother of Jeremy Smith. We don't know for sure whether he is in the hospital or not. I've got kids from that bus wreck out over three different hospitals. I'm gonna go find, find out who we've got here and if he isn't here, we're gonna find out where he is. Okay. But right now, what I need for you to do is just to sit with, uh, Katherine for a little, a little while. Keep her company. Uh, while, while I find out what's going on. Okay?

MIMI 2.1:	Hi Katherine. I'm Mimi. I am the psych. intern here. And I'm going to sit here with you until Dr. James comes back with some information about your son. Is that okay?

KATHERINE 2.13:	You don't have to stay. I mean, I'm alright. I'm not gonna. I mean, I'm not gonna do anything.

MIMI 2.2:	I know, but sometimes, it's just nicer to sit with two instead of by yourself.

KATHERINE 2.14:	Are you a doctor?

MIMI 2.3:	No, I am an intern here at the hospital.

Dick uses a combination of collaborative and direct levels of intervention during this exchange. He realizes that the severity of Katherine's affective, behavioral, and cognitive reactions are high and she is in a state of extreme disequilibrium. Dick works to reassure her that he will do whatever he can in her behalf. He also orchestrates the situation so that he can be confident that Katherine will not do anything that could make things worse.

Step 3: Providing Support

This segment takes place 10 to 15 minutes after the previous one. Dick returns with news that Katherine's son has been admitted into this hospital. However, at the moment Jeremy, Katherine's son, is having surgery to remove a ruptured spleen. This news causes Katherine to begin castastrophizing. Her emotional reaction increases and she begins blaming herself for what happened. This emotional roller coaster experience is common when working with clients in crisis. One moment they are relatively calm and the next moment they are extremely emotional again.

Observe the manner in which Dick responds to Katherine's emotional flare-up. Watch how he remains unruffled and does not argue with Katherine about who is to blame. His focus remains on Katherine and providing her a safe context to vent her feelings. Dick also is careful not to make promises or provide medical information that he is not qualified to give. In these situations it is very tempting to want to say something that will soothe and pacify clients. However, you must keep in mind the limitations of your knowledge and not give information that is misleading or untruthful.

Katherine = Mother
        Dick = Psychologist
        Mimi = Intern

DICK 3.1:   Thank you Mimi.

MIMI 3.1:   Sure. Bye Katherine.

KATHERINE 3.1:   Bye.

DICK 3.2:   Okay, here's what I found out Katherine. We do have your son in the hospital. Um, he's up in the, uh, operating room right now. (pause) What's happening as far as I can understand is this. They brought him in. Uh, the emergency room determined that he had, uh a ruptured spleen. They've got him in the operating room right now and they are working on, on him.

KATHERINE 3.2:   Is he gonna die?

DICK 3.3:   Right now, he is in serious condition. Is he gonna, gonna die? I can't answer that question. It's a serious condition.

KATHERINE 3.3:   (crying) He's my only child. He's my only child. I went through three miscarriages to get him and now he's gonna die on me?

DICK 3.4:   Katherine.

KATHERINE 3.4:   Oh my god, it's my fault.

DICK 3.5:   I want you to, I want you to hear me real carefully. There's no (pause while Katherine is sobbing) Katherine.

KATHERINE 3.5:   No, No, NO! (crying) He's my whole life. (crying)

DICK 3.6:   Katherine.

KATHERINE 3.6:   (crying) He's my whole life.

DICK 3.7:   Katherine. That's, that's horrible news and it's scaring you to death. But he is stable and they are working on him right now. Okay?

KATHERINE 3.7:   (crying) Why didn't somebody tell me? I was at the emergency room. I was standing at the counter. I asked them what, what's going on with my kid? Why didn't they tell me he was in surgery?

DICK 3.8:   Because, right now. They did not know that. Right now, that's where this is.

KATHERINE 3.8:   I, I, I, (crying) oh, god. No ones there for him. He'll never forgive me.

DICK 3.9:   You're right there, right now. (pause while Katherine is crying). I want to know if there is anyone that we need to get a hold of.

64

KATHERINE 3.9:   No, no. My husband's on a trip. He is a pilot. And he's on a trip. He's like, I don't know, shit. East Bajesus, Kuwait or some place like that. He's . . . oh, great! He'll probably get shot down over there. I already got enough stress because of his whole fucking job. Now I've got . . . this. (crying)

DICK 3.10:   Okay, it seems like this is all, all, coming, coming down all - it's like an avalanche. But what I want to do, is I wanna, I wanna get this one little, one little piece for you so you can manage right, right now. Do you hear me when I'm, when I'm saying that your son isn't - death is not imminent. He is in serious condition and they are working on him. He's stabilized; do you hear, hear that?

KATHERINE 3.10:   Yeah.

DICK 3.11:   Okay. Okay.

KATHERINE 3.11:   Yeah.

DICK 3.12:   Now, what I need to do, is I need for you to let me know who I can get here for support. You said that your husband is overseas?

KATHERINE 3.12:   Yeah, he's a pilot.

DICK 3.13:   Okay, we can, I think we can get through to him if you can give me his name and, and his duty station. Is, would you want to talk with him?

KATHERINE 3.13:   I can't tell him this.

DICK 3.14:   Okay. What we can do is that we can do this together.

KATHERINE 3.14:   Will you tell him?

DICK 3.15:   I want, I want you to be there with me. And I want you to talk to him. But I will be there with you.

KATHERINE 3.15:   Okay, okay (crying).

DICK 3.16:   Alright. Now, I want to know if there is anyone around, around here that can be with you right now. I am going to be with you 'til, 'til we get this - he comes out of surgery. I'm gonna keep you updated about what goes on. But I wonder if you got any, anybody here any relatives, any friends, anybody else that can come here and, and be with you.

KATHERINE 3.16:   We just moved here.

DICK 3.17:   Okay.

KATHERINE 3.17:   I don't know anybody. I mean, we literally had been here only about a month and a half - two months. This is a whole new experience for Jeremy to go to this school.

DICK 3.18:	Okay. Would this be alright? We have a group of people here that work, work as volunteers in a hospital. I, I really want someone to be with, with you and be here for you to be able to do things for you to help you, to help you out. Because we're gonna give you a lot of information. We're gonna need to do a lot of different things.
KATHERINE 3.18:	Okay. Okay.
DICK 3.19:	Would you want, would you want, would it be alright if, if for just a little while, I kind of assign Mimi to you - that was in here?
KATHERINE 3.19:	That was the girl that was . . .
DICK 3.20:	. . . that was just in here, that's right. And we can keep her with you for as long as we need to do that.
KATHERINE 3.20:	Can she find out what's going on with my son?
DICK 3.21:	She'll, she'll be in contact with me and I will be in contact with the doctors. And we'll let, we'll let you know immediately when we get any news.
KATHERINE 3.21:	Okay. Okay.
DICK 3.22:	Now, this is going to take a little, a little while, I mean, as I said, this is serious. Okay.
KATHERINE 3.22:	Okay.

Dick's focus in this segment changes from managing Katherine's affective reaction to supporting her as she absorbs the news that her son is in surgery. He recognizes the danger of her spiraling out of control and works to enhance her coping resources. To prevent this situation from occurring, Dick sets into motion a process that encourages Katherine to become temporarily dependent on him. Allowing clients to become dependent is sometimes necessary in crisis intervention. This dependency should be cultivated for clients too vulnerable or unable to care for themselves. Dick recognizes Katherine's reactions are so severe that a direct level of intervention is needed, moving Katherine to become temporarily dependent on him.

Step 4: Examining Alternatives

As this segment begins, Dick is working with Katherine about contacting her husband. The decision has been made that contacting her husband is the first thing Katherine must do. Katherine's unthinking compliance with Dick's directions suggests that her ability to make decisions is compromised. Although Katherine is seemingly calm at the moment, Dick understands that she could suddenly erupt with out-of-control feelings, thoughts, and behaviors. To prevent this situation from happening, Dick continues to promote Katherine's dependency on him.

This step in the systematic model is particularly dependent on the severity of clients' reactions and the crisis situation. Generally speaking, the more severe the reactions the less time this step takes because the options for clients with severe reactions is frequently more limited than for those with mild to moderate reactions. The timing of the event, the event itself, and the options available at that moment also influence the amount of time needed in this step. Any one of these can limit the alternatives that can be generated to resolve a crisis. In Katherine's situation, the hospital setting and nature of her son's injuries restrict the available alternatives.

Observe Dick's attitude as he works with Katherine in this segment. Pay attention to how he takes control of the situation, yet also ensures that Katherine is part of the process.

Key: **Katherine = Mother**
        Dick = Psychologist

DICK 4.1:	Now, what I need to do is I'm, I'm, I'm need for you to let me know who I can get here to support. You said your husband is overseas?
KATHERINE 4.1:	Yeah, he's a pilot.
DICK 4.2:	Okay. We can, I think we can, we can get through to him if you can give me his name and, and, and his duty station. Is, would you want to talk with him?
KATHERINE 4.2:	I can't tell him this.
DICK 4.3:	Okay. What we can do is that we can do this together.
KATHERINE 4.3:	Will you tell him?
DICK 4.4:	I want I want you to be there with me. And I want you to talk to him. But I'll be there with you.
KATHERINE 4.4:	Okay.

In this segment, Dick allows Katherine to be involved in the process, yet does not force the involvement beyond her ability to cope at that moment. He walks a fine line, balancing Katherine's need to be dependent on him with the need for her to feel in control. Effective crisis intervention often calls for this approach. Crisis workers must be careful not to inappropriately manipulate or take advantage of clients who are as needy as Katherine. Dick does this by maintaining an appropriate professional boundary as he helps Katherine prepare to contact her husband.

Step 5: Making Plans

Making the plan to contact Katherine's husband is the primary focus of this segment. Dick takes an active role as he helps Katherine organize her thoughts and manage immediate concerns. He makes the crisis manageable by helping Katherine organize the crisis into small pieces that can be handled in the short-term. Systematically, Dick helps Katherine think about her day and identify anything that must be done. This process taxes Katherine's fragile coping skills, resulting in Dick assuming the responsibility for taking care of these concerns. Given the severity of Katherine's reactions this situation is typical, especially if the client has a minimal support system.

As the segment progresses, observe Katherine's inability to perform simple tasks or recall information. She relies on Dick as she struggles to locate identification information for her husband and remember where she is employed. Also notice the manner in which Dick supports and validates Katherine's reactions.

DICK 5.1:   Do you want, do you want me to go ahead and start the ball rolling to get, to get in touch with your husband?

KATHERINE 5.1:   Yeah.

DICK 5.2:   Okay?

KATHERINE 5.2:   Yeah.

DICK 5.3:   Alright. I'm gonna, I'm gonna do that. Um, I'm gonna need for you to give me his um, uh, duty station, and, and his full rank, serial number and so on and so forth. Okay?

KATHERINE 5.3:   Okay.

DICK 5.4:   Alright.

KATHERINE 5.4:   I'm even using his wallet. (crying) My whole life is just falling apart. Every time I turn around there is something else going on.

DICK 5.5:   I'm sure, it seems, it seems like that right now, but we're gonna, we're gonna keep . . .

KATHERINE 5.5:   God damn it! Shit!

DICK 5.6:   Okay.

KATHERINE 5.6:   Ugh!

DICK 5.7:   Okay, just calm down. Can you just calm down?

KATHERINE 5.7:   Oh, here just find it, just find the damn thing. It's the Navy.

DICK 5.8:   Okay. Alright. Alright. What I'm gonna do is I'm gonna go ahead and do this. I'm gonna get a, I will check and see. Get another report. I want to assure you that as soon as we find out anything, uh, about your son I'm gonna tell you when he gets out of operating, we're gonna take you up in, up there and we're gonna take you in recovery. Okay? And you'll be, be there when he comes, comes out from, uh, uh, out of anesthetic, okay?

KATHERINE 5.8:   How long is he gonna be in the hospital?

DICK 5.9:   I can't tell you that, I don't know. Uh, he certainly will be here for awhile. And, uh, we're gonna, we'll make arrangements to work with you, and setting up a place for you here, here to be with him, to sleep here and what, whatever you need. We can do that.

KATHERINE 5.9:   I'm so alone.

DICK 5.10:	Okay. And I'm sorry that you have no, no one here, here else but what we're gonna our best here at the hospital is to support you in every possible way that we can. I know that's not your family, I know that's not your husband. But, um, uh, rest assure that you're gonna have support here. And we're gonna, we're gonna to do what's needed to be done, uh, to see that, uh, Jeremy gets well and, uh, that you get all of the information that you need. What I need for you to do right now, uh, is be exactly what you are doing right now. Is to be, to be strong and be supportive and be ready just to take care of your son when he comes out of surgery. Katherine, I've said a lot of things to you, um, but what I need to know right now is what do you need to have happen that we can, we can keep you, let you here at the hospital. I'm kind of wondering about your job or any other kind of responsibilities that you have.
KATHERINE 5.10:	Oh, my god, my job. I have a job. I have to go, I have to go, I have to go to my job.
DICK 5.11:	Okay.
KATHERINE 5.11:	I have to . . . but,
DICK 5.12:	Okay, Katherine I understand that, that, that, that's another thing that I've just added to your life. But, but, hold on, hold on just a second. Okay?
KATHERINE 5.12:	What am I gonna tell them? I can't leave here. I can't. What am I supposed to do?
DICK 5.13:	Okay, we're gonna take care of that. Where, where do you work?
KATHERINE 5.13:	Uh, it's a new job. It's a brand new job.
DICK 5.14:	Take your time.
KATHERINE 5.14:	Jesus, it's a brand new job. I mean, I should know where I work, christ.
DICK 5.15:	That's okay, take your time. You've been under a tremendous amount of stress. And probably the last thing on your mind is where you work right now. Okay, it's a new job, I understand that.
KATHERINE 5.15:	God. Um. It's that new graphic design place that's downtown, that, that's on uh, on . . . Washington St. No! Jefferson, Jefferson. Johnson. Johnson's Graphics Designs. That's it, god, shit.
DICK 5.16:	Alright. What we're gonna do is we're gonna call Johnson's Graphics Design. Okay. And we're gonna tell them the problem. But is there anything that you want us to tell them because what we're gonna say to them is where you are, what's going on.
KATHERINE 5.16:	I don't know. I don't know, I don't know what to do. I don't know what to tell them, I mean. I don't know how they're going to take this, I mean, what am I supposed to do?

DICK 5.17:	Okay, what I'm going to do is I'm going, I'm going to call them up. Okay? I'm going to tell them that your son's in the hospital here, that he's undergone an operation, this is a serious one and you're here at the hospital. I'll get some information on, on them about, about that. Is there any particular person that you wish me to ask for down there.
KATHERINE 5.17:	Um, (pause), just (pause), um (pause). Frank.
DICK 5.18:	Frank?
KATHERINE 5.18:	Frank Johnson is the owner.
DICK 5.19:	Okay.
KATHERINE 5.19:	He should, he should be there I think?
DICK 5.20:	Alright, then that's what I'll, what I'll do. Okay? How about your home. How did, how did you get here Katherine?
KATHERINE 5.20:	I drove.
DICK 5.21:	Okay. Is there, is there anything we need to, need to do about your home?
KATHERINE 5.21:	I threw my keys in the emergency room I don't know where they went. I can't get home because I don't know where my fucking keys are.
DICK 5.22:	Okay. Then if, we'll, we'll launch a search for your keys. Um, and if we can't, find, find that we'll, we'll get somebody out, out here to get your car, car open. I need to know too, if it's okay, if I've got your permission to go ahead and make that call now to, uh, Mr. Johnson.
KATHERINE 5.22:	Yeah.
DICK 5.23:	Can I do that? And tell him where you are?
KATHERINE 5.23:	You're going to call my husband.
DICK 5.24:	Yes we will. I, I don't quite how long that's going to take but we're, we're gonna start the ball rolling immediately. And, and see if we can't get through to him, okay?

Two important processes take place in this segment. First, Dick carefully outlines for Katherine the information he has regarding the condition of her son and the plan to see him as soon as possible. Whereas this process may be redundant, clients in crisis may need to be given information repeatedly. Repeating this information is critical to keep Katherine calm and allow her to regain a sense of control. As you may recall, initially the hospital staff was not helpful, causing Katherine's already heightened emotions to become even more exaggerated. Second, Dick works with Katherine to develop a plan for the next few hours. He assumes responsibility for taking care of several routine tasks for Katherine. Notice that as he takes these responsibilities, Dick is attentive to ethical guidelines such as confidentiality and obtains verbal permission to contact her place of employment.

Step 6: Obtaining Commitment

In this final segment, Dick checks to determine that Katherine has an understanding of the plan. As he discusses the plan, he also writes it down to make certain Katherine has something concrete to refer to at a later time. Again, the repetition is extremely important since Katherine's ability to retain information is compromised. Dick senses the need to monitor Katherine during these next few critical hours; therefore, he assigns the psychology intern to stay with her. Having the psychology intern with her achieves two goals. First, it ensures that Katherine is attending to issues such as eating and resting, and second, the psychology intern can alert Dick if Katherine begins to lose control again.

Notice the length of Dick's responses in this segment as opposed to Katherine's responses. Katherine's exhaustion is easily seen as she can manage mostly one word responses. Also pay attention to the topics Dick discusses. In addition to recapping the plan, he encourages Katherine to take care of herself.

Key: **Katherine = Mother**
Dick = Psychologist

DICK 6.1:	The most important thing right, right now is for you to be with your son and get through this. And we're going to support you in every, every which way possible. Is, is there anything else that you can think of right now that we need to do?
KATHERINE 6.1:	No.
DICK 6.2:	Okay. And again, this might seem really, really kind of tedious, but I am going to write all of this stuff down, okay? We're going to put together just a little plan here. And you and I are going to see that so, so we can, we can keep track of all this stuff. Alright? When I get done, done here, I'm going us to go do this. I'm going to have Mimi come back in here, okay? And, and then, as, as soon as Jeremy gets out of the operating room, I'm going to take you right upstairs. Okay? You've got to trust us on, on this. You don't need to be up there right now, but, but we'll get you up there just as soon as he comes, comes out. Okay?
KATHERINE 6.2:	Okay.
DICK 6.3:	Okay. What I want you to do, can you look at me right now? Can you get your eyes with me? Is there anything about this that I've said that you don't understand?
KATHERINE 6.3:	No.
DICK 6.4:	Okay, if you could, just kind of briefly, just so I'm, I feel assured about this, that you're okay. Can you tell me what we've talked about and what we're gonna, what we're gonna do. Just take your time.
KATHERINE 6.4:	You're gonna call my work. You're gonna find my husband. And you're gonna take me up to see my kid.

DICK 6.5:	That's right. And as soon as I get your husband on the line, you and I are going to talk, talk with him. Okay?
KATHERINE 6.5:	Okay.
DICK 6.6:	Alright. And, and then we'll sit down and we'll talk, we'll talk a little about what we're going to say to him. Because, right now, we really don't know all we are going to say to him because that will depend a lot on how, on how Jeremy is when he comes out of the operating room. Okay?
KATHERINE 6.6:	Okay.
DICK 6.7:	Alright, I'm going to get Mimi, she's going to come back in here. And I'm, I'm going to get the ball rolling on this.
KATHERINE 6.7:	Okay.
DICK 6.8:	Alright? Okay. It's tough, but you're doing a good job with it. You stay, you stay right with it. We'll get through this I'll be back in here just as soon as I find, find this out. But it will, it will take a little time. If you need anything to eat, anything to drink, and I know you saying, "Nah". But, but if you, if you do, we want, we want to keep you in physically good shape. And being there for your son is the best thing you can do right now, okay?
KATHERINE 6.8:	Okay.

This segment serves as a summary of everything that took place as Dick helped Katherine absorb the news that her son had been injured in an accident. A focal point of the segment is involving Katherine as much as possible. However given her current state, the involvement is limited. Therefore, Dick continues to promote Katherine's dependence on him but continually assesses Katherine's ability to reclaim her independence. He does this through encouragement and enjoining her to take care of herself.

CASE TWO: The Anxious Father

The case of the Anxious Father, Hassan, involves his need to spend time with his children. Hassan is divorced and his former wife is refusing to allow him to see the children. The reason for her inflexibility is that Hassan has not paid child support for several months. Hassan explains that the lapse in child support payments is because he lost his job and he simply does not have the money at this time. A complication to the current crisis is that Hassan is a recovering addict. He has been clean for over three years but is now thinking about using again. Although he knows using drugs again is not in his best interest, the pain of not seeing his children is so great he is beginning to think he has no other way to ease the pain.

The session takes place at the outpatient drug rehabilitation clinic where Hassan received treatment three years ago. He came back to the clinic to seek advice from his therapist with whom he had a good relationship; however, his former therapist has the day off. Recognizing his desperate state, the receptionist immediately arranges for Hassan to see another therapist.

Step 1: Defining the Problem

As the session begins, Hassan is very anxious. Rick begins slowly by validating Hassan's feelings and gathering basic information. This process helps Rick assess Hassan's current state and determine that he is not using drugs at the moment. Establishing this fact is critical for helping clients in crisis. If Hassan had been high on drugs, the session would have focused on giving support to Hassan as he came down off the drugs rather than helping to resolve the crisis. In this segment Hassan identifies several problems: (a) thoughts of using drugs again; (b) loss of job; (c) potential loss of his house; and (d) not having contact with his children. Although these are all related, Rick must sort through the confusion to understand Hassan's crisis.

Observe the effect Rick's non-threatening approach has on Hassan as the segment progresses. Note the types of questions Rick asked and the effect these had on Hassan. Also, pay attention to the non-verbal behaviors that help Rick conclude Hassan is not using at the moment.

Key: Hassan = Father
    Rick = Psychologist

RICK 1.1:	Hi, my name's Rick.
HASSAN 1.1:	Hi. I, I need to see Ed Jones. I need to see him right away.
RICK 1.2:	Yeah, yeah just a second. What's your name again?
HASSAN 1.2:	My name is Hassan.
RICK 1.3:	Hassan?
HASSAN 1.3:	Yes. I need to talk to Ed Jones.
RICK 1.4:	Ed Jones.
HASSAN 1.4:	Is he here today?
RICK 1.5:	Well, he's not here today but the receptionist said that you needed to talk to someone right away.
HASSAN 1.5:	Yes, I need, I need to talk . . . is Ed here?
RICK 1.6:	No, he's not here but maybe I can help you. Um, why don't you sit down and we can see what's going on.
HASSAN 1.6:	Alright, alright. And, who are you?
RICK 1.7:	My name is Rick.
HASSAN 1.7:	Okay.
RICK 1.8:	And now, Ed Jones. Who's Ed Jones?
HASSAN 1.8:	Ed Jones is my therapist. I, I saw him about three years ago. I, I need to talk to, I need to talk to him right now.

RICK 1.9:	Right now?
HASSAN 1.9:	Right now. I have a lot of stuff going on. Um, I just need to talk to him.
RICK 1.10:	Yeah, you seem pretty anxious right now. What's going on?
HASSAN 1.10:	I, I just need to talk to him. I can't . . . my wife said that I can never see my kids, I, I lost my job, I have no money, I can't take care of my house. I just need to, I need to talk to Ed, he really helped me out.
RICK 1.11:	Yeah, lots of stuff is happening to you right now.
HASSAN 1.11:	Yes.
RICK 1.12:	A lot of stuff out of control.
HASSAN 1.12:	Yes.
RICK 1.13:	Yeah. Now, when did you come in before?
HASSAN 1.13:	Ah, it was about three years ago.
RICK 1.14:	About three years ago?
HASSAN 1.14:	Yes.
RICK 1.15:	And what were you in for treatment three years ago?
HASSAN 1.15:	I, I was using three years ago.
RICK 1.16:	Yeah?
HASSAN 1.16:	Yeah.
RICK 1.17:	What were you using?
HASSAN 1.17:	I was, um, smoking mixed blunts. Doing powdered cocaine. Um, you know, drinking, drinking a lot, so.
RICK 1.18:	Okay.
HASSAN 1.18:	Really bad off.
RICK 1.19:	Okay.
HASSAN 1.19:	I've been clean. . . ever since then.
RICK 1.20:	Yeah.
HASSAN 1.20:	I don't know what I'm gonna do now.

RICK 1.21:	Yeah. So you're not using now is what you are saying.
HASSAN 1.21:	Right. I don't know what I'm gonna do though. I'm, I'm . . . I wanna . . . I, I just don't know. I got so much stuff going on. Can't see my kids, I lost my job.
RICK 1.22:	Yeah. Yeah. It sounds like Ed was helpful to you.
HASSAN 1.22:	Yeah, very helpful.
RICK 1.23:	Yeah. Yeah. Yeah, well Ed's not here today. So, uh . . .
HASSAN 1.23:	Where is he?
RICK 1.24:	Well, this is his day off.
HASSAN 1.24:	Oh.
RICK 1.25:	And I wondering if maybe you just like to just tell me what's going on.
HASSAN 1.25:	I don't, I don't know. I just so much going on right. I can't see my kids. I don't have a job. Um, I can't take care of my house. Um, you know, it's just, my life is a mess.
RICK 1.26:	Well, it sounds like a lot of stuff's happening to you. Let's slow down here. Which thing seems to be the most important to you right now?
HASSAN 1.26:	Uhh, everything is important to me, I mean . . .
RICK 1.27:	Yeah.
HASSAN 1.27:	Everything's in a . . . I gotta . . . I don't know what I'm gonna do.
RICK 1.28:	Yeah.
HASSAN 1.28:	I think about using . . . you know.
RICK 1.29:	Wait, wait. You're thinking about using again?
HASSAN 1.29:	Yeah.
RICK 1.30:	Yeah.
HASSAN 1.30:	I could really go for something right now.
RICK 1.31:	It would calm you down, it sounds like.
HASSAN 1.31:	Yeah.
RICK 1.32:	Yeah. Well, you know, I think that maybe there's some things that we can work on together that can help calm you down, uh, so that you don't use again. You've been clean?

HASSAN 1.32:   Yes, I've been clean.

RICK 1.33:   You got a sponsor?

HASSAN 1.33:   Yes, I do.

RICK 1.34:   Have you talk to the sponsor lately?

HASSAN 1.34:   Nah, my life has just been hectic. Uh . . . you know, I want to see my kids.

RICK 1.35:   Okay. Have you been going to any meetings or anything?

HASSAN 1.35:   No.

RICK 1.36:   No?

HASSAN 1.36:   No.

RICK 1.37:   No. Okay, okay, but you want to see your kids. You keep bringing up your kids. What's, tell me about what's happened with that.

HASSAN 1.37:   My wife's said that I can never see my kids ever again.

RICK 1.38:   That sounds kind of final.

HASSAN 1.38:   Yeah, she does that.

RICK 1.39:   And I kind of get the hunch that your kids are important to you.

HASSAN 1.39:   Yes they are.

RICK 1.40:   Yeah.

HASSAN 1.40:   Very important.

RICK 1.41:   Yeah. How many kids do you have?

HASSAN 1.41:   I have two.

RICK 1.42:   Two?

HASSAN 1.42:   Yes.

RICK 1.43:   How old are they?

HASSAN 1.43:   Five and seven.

RICK 1.44:   Yeah. Yeah.

HASSAN 1.44:   (Pause) I don't know what I'm going to do.

RICK 1.45:   Yeah, I'm hearing that.

Although Hassan wanted to see the therapist he had seen previously, Rick is able to establish rapport. The process of gaining trust was straightforward because of Hassan's sense of disequilibrium. However given Hassan's history, Rick proceeds in a measured way. Two different types of questions are used to help relieve Hassan's anxiety. First, Rick asks questions about attending meetings and the sponsors that Hassan would expect if he returned to the place he received treatment for drug use. Rick also asked questions requiring simple responses to help ease Hassan's anxiety. Combined, these questions began the process of sorting through Hassan's confusion in order to resolve the crisis.

Step 2: Safety

A few minutes elapse prior to the beginning of this segment. Rick has worked to reduce Hassan's anxiety. Hassan is now less anxious allowing Rick to focus on ensuring Hassan's safety. In this situation, this means ensuring Hassan does not start using drugs again.

Pay attention to the directness and intention of Rick's questions. These questions straightforwardly ask about Hassan's intention and also build on the strength he has displayed in the past. Rick is very direct in telling Hassan to use that strength to stay clean.

Key: Hassan = Father
**   Rick = Psychologist**

HASSAN 2.1:   (sigh) Man.

RICK 2.1:   Yeah. Let's, let's take a breath now. I know you're anxious. Tell me about this wanting to use again. Um, what can you tell me about that?

HASSAN 2.2:   I want to go smoke a blunt right now.

RICK 2.2:   Yeah. I'd kind of be surprised if you didn't want to go smoke a blunt right now.

HASSAN 2.3:   And a few other things too, but.

RICK 2.3:   Yeah? You need something to calm you down.

HASSAN 2.4:   Yeah, I need something to take this pain away.

RICK 2.4:   Pain away. Okay. What, what's kept you from using in the past four years?

HASSAN 2.5:   I mean, you know. Being around . . . you know, it's my whole environment. Being able to work, being able to talk to positive people. Working the program. But now, it doesn't matter anymore, I can't see my kids.

RICK 2.5:   Um, man, it just feels like you trying to juggle too many things all at once. And I need to get a commitment from you right now. Uh, if you see your kids, you're not going to use, right?

HASSAN 2.6:   Yeah!

RICK 2.6:   Are you sure about that?

HASSAN 2.7:	I'm positive if I see my kids.
RICK 2.7:	Yeah, that's, that's the one thing that you can hold onto to keep you from using right now.
HASSAN 2.8:	Right.
RICK 2.8:	Okay.

In this brief exchange Hassan's temptation to use drugs is addressed. Rick obtains a promise from Hassan to not use again. This promise is believable because Hassan has stayed clean for four years and sought help to avoid using again. Rick also could have developed a "non-use" contract with Hassan, although he chose not to. A non-use contract is similar to the non-suicide contract we discussed in Section Three, except the content would address not using drugs.

Step 3: Providing Support

In this segment, Rick provides support by reframing the crisis in terms Hassan understands and by pointing out that he has the basic skills to resolve the crisis. Although Hassan is skeptical initially, he concedes Rick is correct as the segment progresses. Rick also questions Hassan about the strength he used getting and staying clean. He points out that he can use that same strength to work through the crisis. This thought had never occurred to Hassan. He had developed tunnel vision and was not able to see beyond the immediacy of his desire to spend time with his children. Combined, seeing the crisis from a different perspective and using a strength-based approach supplies Hassan with the encouragement he needs to resolve the crisis.

Pay attention to Hassan's non-verbal behavior as the segment progresses. Especially note the decrease in movement that suggests he is becoming less anxious. Observe Rick as he partners with Hassan, helping Hassan develop a renewed sense of confidence.

Key: **Hassan = Father**
Rick = Psychologist

RICK 3.1:	Now, you know, as I'm thinking about this, you said, you said you were an engineer?
HASSAN 3.1:	Yes.
RICK 3.2:	Yeah. What kind of an engineer?
HASSAN 3.2:	Electrical.
RICK 3.3:	Yeah. How, uh, went to school to learn about that and that kind of stuff. And, you probably learned how to solve problems.
HASSAN 3.3:	Yeah.
RICK 3.4:	Well, you know, I'm just wondering if maybe we can use some of the stuff you learned being an engineer to solve this problem. Kind of engineer the problem.

78

HASSAN 3.4:	Wow. Yeah we could.
RICK 3.5:	Okay. What's the problem that you see right now?
HASSAN 3.5:	I can't see my kids.
RICK 3.6:	You can't see your kids.
HASSAN 3.6:	Right.
RICK 3.7:	Yeah, that's. You know, I don't know that that's the problem. (pause)
HASSAN 3.7:	Why not?
RICK 3.8:	Kind of surprised you, huh? Yeah. I think the problem's your wife.
HASSAN 3.8:	Oh yes, she's part of that.
RICK 3.9:	Well, what, what's she telling you about not seeing your kids. Why, why is she saying that you can't see your kids?
HASSAN 3.9:	Cuz, I, you know, jeopardy of losing my house, uh, you know, I'm not working. I don't have any money to, you know, pay child support. All of those things.
RICK 3.10:	Okay. Okay, let's, let's take one of these at a time. Let's, let's kind of list out the problems here. She's not letting . . . I mean, the reasons she's giving you for not seeing your kids. You lost your job.
HASSAN 3.10:	Right. (nodding)
RICK 3.11:	You have, uh, you haven't been paying child support as a result.
HASSAN 3.11:	Right.
RICK 3.12:	Um, is that, is that, are those the two reasons?
HASSAN 3.12:	And I, and my house. Cuz, they have no place to stay if I lose my house. Cuz she knows that I am in jeopardy of losing my house.
RICK 3.13:	Oh, okay. So you're behind on your house payments too. So, you might get asked to leave. Now, do you own the house or are you renting the house?
HASSAN 3.13:	I own the house.
RICK 3.14:	Okay you own the house or you're buying the house.
HASSAN 3.14:	Yeah, buying it. Yeah, yeah.
RICK 3.15:	Well, let's look at these each individually and let's see if we can engineer a way . . . figure out a way to solve these . . . so that you can go to your wife

and show her that you're really trying. And I'm thinking that together we can engineer something that's going to be helpful to remove that obstacle and I'm wondering if your willing to buy into that.

HASSAN 3.15:   I want to do something cause I know that I'm going to use again.

RICK 3.16:   Yeah, yeah.

HASSAN 3.16:   I want to do something right now.

RICK 3.17:   And the goal is to keep from getting into pissin' matches with your wife when you talk to her. So what I want to do is use just some basic communication kinds of stuff. Almost like communication engineering. To be able to um, help you talk with your wife in a straight forward way and not start bringing in all this other stuff that's probably not all that relevant.

HASSAN 3.17:   Alright.

RICK 3.18:   Okay?

HASSAN 3.18:   Yeah.

RICK 3.19:   Sounds like a, like an idea.

HASSAN 3.19:   Yes, sounds like an idea. Yeah. It's just hard.

RICK 3.20:   It is hard. I understand that. But, you've done hard stuff before.

HASSAN 3.20:   Yeah.

RICK 3.21:   My guess, my guess is that getting clean was pretty hard.

HASSAN 3.21:   Yes it was. Remaining clean is even harder.

RICK 3.22:   Yeah. Staying clean is even harder. And you've been doing that for four years now?

HASSAN 3.22:   Yeah.

RICK 3.23:   So you can do hard stuff.

HASSAN 3.23:   Yeah. (nodding) I can do it.

RICK 3.24:   You can do hard stuff, yeah.

Rick uses strategies in this segment that help Hassan regain a sense of control. Feeling out of control is common for someone in crisis. Rick knows that before resolving the crisis, Hassan needs to believe he has some control over his life. By identifying several of Hassan's strengths, Rick begins the process of helping him recover that control. Although much has already been accomplished, Hassan has only taken the first important step to resolving the crisis.

Step 4: Examining Alternatives

Fifteen minutes have elapsed as this segment begins. Hassan is stuck attempting to figure out a way to approach his former wife. He desperately wants to spend time with his children but is caught in a vicious cycle of repetitive thinking. He is mired in a train of thought believing the only way he can resolve the crisis is to pay the child support. His frustration is evident and he is at the point of trying anything that can help. Hassan's receptiveness to using a novel approach is a sign of the severity of his reactions. Generally speaking, the more the severe the reaction the more receptive clients are to attempting a different approach. Rick plays a hunch that every time Hassan and his wife talk, they argue. The hunch is accurate and breaks through Hassan's myopic view of the way to resolve the crisis. Using Hassan's background in engineering, Rick and Hassan are able to work toward a resolution of the crisis.

Observe Rick's focus on Hassan's strengths in this segment. Notice the way Rick demonstrates to Hassan that he is listening while consistently pushing Hassan toward a positive frame of mind.

Key: **Hassan = Father**
Rick = Psychologist

HASSAN 4.1:	I gotta show her something . . .I mean, I gotta show her that I can pay something.
RICK 4.1:	Okay.
HASSAN 4.2:	Child support or whatever.
RICK 4.2:	Okay, well, you know, it's gonna help me. . . I know it's kind of going back. When your conversations with her over the past couple of weeks, couple of months, what have they, what have they been like?
HASSAN 4.3:	Not too good. She's very upset. She's not receiving child support. Um, I mean, she said I'm not doing what I am supposed to be doing. So . . .
RICK 4.3:	She sounds angry.
HASSAN 4.4:	Very angry.
RICK 4.4:	Yeah. Okay. So, that's . . .we got to figure how to get around that anger.
HASSAN 4.5:	I don't know if we can. I mean, if she comes over and says, "Can I bum some money?" and I say, "Here".
RICK 4.5:	What, what's making her angry, though.
HASSAN 4.6:	Child support.
RICK 4.6:	The child support. Okay. Well, right now your, your . . . you just said a few minutes ago that your unemployment is going to kick in pretty soon.

HASSAN 4.7:	Yeah, well, it's already started kicking in but still . . . I mean, it's taken out but it's still not enough. The way everything's calculated and. . . the lay offs and all that stuff, so.
RICK 4.7:	You know. Hassan, I may be wrong, and correct me if I am. But my guess is, that when you get to talking with your wife, when you contact her, you get angry, she gets angry. You make demands, she refuses and it just kind of goes out of control. Kind of spins out of control.
HASSAN 4.8:	Yeah, we get in a pissin' match.
RICK 4.8:	Yeah, okay. Yeah, well, I'm maybe thinking about one of the things that we can engineer to help you with is to help you learn how to approach her that's not quite so aggressive, so demanding.
HASSAN 4.9:	Well, I want to see my kids.
RICK 4.9:	Yeah, I know. I know. I am hearing that. And I want to help you to see your kids. But it sounds like what you've been doing to try to see your kids hasn't been, hasn't been helping a whole lot.
HASSAN 4.10:	No.
RICK 4.10:	No. So I'm wondering if maybe trying a new approach to talking with her, to talk, to discussing you know, what's going on in your life might be more helpful. Instead of making demand - "I need, I want to see my kids!" There might be another way to approach her that, uh, might diffuse her anger.
HASSAN 4.11:	I don't know. You don't know her. (laughing)
RICK 4.11:	I don't know her?
HASSAN 4.12:	I don't know how to, if there is another way to approach her but I'm willing to hear.
RICK 4.12:	Yeah. Sounds like a tough person.
HASSAN 4.13:	Yeah, she is.
RICK 4.13:	Yeah, sounds like you're a pretty committed person though, to seeing your kids.
HASSAN 4.14:	Yes, I am.
RICK 4.14:	And my guess is that you've handled a lot of tough problems in engineering.
HASSAN 4.15:	Right, but those are -- it's either this or that or you know, there's ways around, you know, making, making things work. But this is, I mean that's tangible.
RICK 4.15:	Well that sounds like. . .

HASSAN 4.16:	Dealing with family. Dealing with feelings.
RICK 4.16:	Yeah, yeah, sounds like though, you had to be creative though, in making things work. Well, let's see if we can be creative here. And I know that maybe you don't have all of the skills to do it, but, maybe I can help you learn some of those, uh, pretty quick, to uh, to help you approach her in ways that will keep you from getting in, what you said a few minutes ago, "a pissin' match".
HASSAN 4.17:	Alright.
RICK 4.17:	Are you willing to do some of that?
HASSAN 4.18:	Yeah, we can look at some of that, but. Yeah, we can do that.
RICK 4.18:	Okay.

Rick recognizes that the way Hassan is approaching the crisis is counter productive. Therefore, Rick challenges Hassan to open his thinking to learning a new coping skill for approaching the crisis. People find it difficult to change their approach to a crisis even though it is not working. When this occurs, crisis workers must introduce the possibility of learning a new skill. However, care must be used to avoid making clients feel inadequate. Rick avoids alienating Hassan by presenting the development of the skills in a familiar context, in this situation, engineering. This prospect intrigues Hassan and allows the process of resolving the crisis to continue.

Step 5: Making a Plan

Rick introduces Hassan to a different approach for talking with his former wife in this segment. Instead of demanding to see the children, Rick encourages him to tell his former wife about his struggles and the support the children give him. Hassan is receptive and able to expand on the message Rick suggests. In addition to talking about his struggles, Rick suggests that Hassan offer his former wife information on his efforts to find a new job. As he talks about his efforts, Hassan seems surprised he has done so much and he regains some confidence. Before the segment ends, Rick asks Hassan to develop a back-up plan in case his former wife is not open to this new approach. A back-up plan is needed in this situation to boost Hassan's chances of success and avoid his feeling of being a failure again.

Pay attention to the process Rick uses to help Hassan understand and learn the new approach to talk with his former wife. Notice that Rick offers a suggestion about what to say and then asks Hassan to use his own words to say the same thing. This process allows Hassan to have control of the situation while Rick makes sure Hassan knows the important part of the message that is to be conveyed to his former wife.

Key:	**Hassan = Father**
	Rick = Psychologist

RICK 5.1:	What is it, the first thing that you want to say to your wife?
HASSAN 5.1:	(laughing) See my kids.
RICK 5.2:	To see your kids. Okay, well let's change that . . . just a little bit. I want to keep the focus on seeing your kids. But, maybe you might want to say

something like, "I know I haven't been keeping up with the child support payments right now, but I really need some moral support. And my kids give me the moral support. And I am wondering if that's possible to be able to see my kids."

HASSAN 5.2:   You want me to say that to her?

RICK 5.3:   Yeah. Well, put it in your own words. Put it in your own words what I just said.

HASSAN 5.3:   Hmm. I guess, um, (pause) alright, um . . . "I haven't been doing what I'm supposed to be doing and, you know, I really want to see my kids. They really help me out a lot".

RICK 5.4:   Okay, okay. Now, my guess is that you've said things like that but I think you're going to need to say a couple of other things to her too. But, how did that feel to you?

HASSAN 5.4:   (laughing) It was kind of difficult.

RICK 5.5:   Kind of difficult? Yeah, I got, got the sense that it was a little bit tough. What was tough about it?

HASSAN 5.5:   Cuz, I don't like to not do what I'm . . . I don't like to be a failure. I feel I'm a failure.

RICK 5.6:   Maybe you want to say, maybe you want to say that to her too? "I don't like being a failure and I feel like I've been failing you by not paying, failing my children, because I haven't been paying the child support. But I need to see them right now so I can get some support and, some, support from them." Okay, you want to say that, what is it? "I felt like I was, I feel . . ."

HASSAN 5.6:   "I feel, I feel like I'm a failure to you and to the children. Cuz, I haven't been doing what I need to do. Be supportive, um, financially. I haven't been there, you know, been able to do that, losing my job."

RICK 5.7:   What else. Though, there was one other little tag to that about, ". . but I need to see my kids because I need that support right now."

HASSAN 5.7:   Yeah. "I need to see my kids cuz, I need that support."

RICK 5.8:   Yeah. I'm wondering also though if you need to tell her, have some facts to give her, because you know, I know engineers like facts. How many resumes do you have out now?

HASSAN 5.8:   Oh, about five. Send out another one here soon I guess. About five, I'm gonna have five out there, five out there.

RICK 5.9:   You have five out there. So I'm wondering if maybe you need to say, "You know, I know you're concerned about me looking for a job, but I have five resumes out there now." Any interviews scheduled or anything?

84

HASSAN 5.9:	No. Not yet.
RICK 5.10:	Not yet?
HASSAN 5.10:	It takes about, you know, almost six months for call-backs and all that stuff, so. I don't know, maybe I will be fortunate and get an interview or something.
RICK 5.11:	Okay, so you don't know. Maybe you can say it, "You know, I have five resumes out there, prospects look good, but it's just going to take awhile. It might take a month or two before things are going to start happening." What other kinds of things have you been doing looking for a job that you can talk to her about?
HASSAN 5.11:	I've been to, you know, the whole you know, that whole, you know, seminar, the "Dislocated Workers" and all that stuff, I mean. Been there, done that. It's not been helpful. The agencies hasn't been helpful.
RICK 5.12:	Yeah, it may not have been helpful, but did you tell her that you did all that stuff?
HASSAN 5.12:	Maybe I have. I don't, I don't, I don't remember if I . . . I don't know how I told her. (laughing) But, I think it came out.
RICK 5.13:	You might have told her in anger or something. She was probably angry so she wasn't listening and neither were you. I'm wondering if maybe, you could remind her. That, "Yeah, I've been to these workshops, or these, you know, these kind of teaching sessions, about helping people who have lost their jobs, been laid-off." To show her that you are working to find something more.
HASSAN 5.13:	Yeah, I can say that to her . . . again.
RICK 5.14:	I'm thinking that, you know, even though we've talked about how, some things that you can say to her, I'm afraid she's still going to get angry.
HASSAN 5.14:	Yeah.
RICK 5.15:	Probably so. Yeah. It would be my guess, wouldn't it?
HASSAN 5.15:	Yeah, yes, yes.
RICK 5.16:	So I'm thinking you need a backup plan. Kind of like in engineering. Do you have back up plans in engineering sometimes?
HASSAN 5.16:	Yes, have to.
RICK 5.17:	Have to have them. Okay, remember, we're kind of engineering this so we need a backup plan. And one of the things you know, I think would be helpful is something called a broken record. I know that doesn't make any sense to you but you need to have something you can say to her when she starts getting angry. Um, like, you know, "I know you're getting angry right

now, but right now I need to see my kids. And I understand that I haven't been doing what I need to do." Um.

HASSAN 5.17:   Say that to her?

RICK 5.18:   Yeah. Well, maybe not in those words. What words would you use?

HASSAN 5.18:   I mean, I know I guess I would say that, "I know this has been difficult for you and for the kids."

RICK 5.19:   Great! That's good.

HASSAN 5.19:   "...and you know, I-I wanna , you know, I do want to see my kids they provide me with some support." And I guess I would just keep saying that in so many words. . . cuz things get escalated, I guess, cuz they do.

RICK 5.20:   Okay. Okay. So, when she gets angry, which she probably will. I mean, that would be my guess from what you've told me about her. I don't know her but she sounds like a tough woman. She's probably going to get pretty pissed at you.

HASSAN 5.20:   Uh huh.

RICK 5.21:   And she might start calling . . . I mean, she's gonna pull out all of the stops. So you can say what?

HASSAN 5.21:   I can say "Hey, you know, I know it's been difficult for you, um you know, throughout this time and you know, I really want to see, to see, to see the kids. And I want to do, you know, what I need to do to see them. You know, I just need that support."

RICK 5.22:   Okay. And for when she starts getting angry. Now I think we need a backup plan for you too for when you start getting angry.

HASSAN 5.22:   (laughing) Yeah, that would be helpful. Cuz, I will probably get angry too.

RICK 5.23:   Probably get angry as well. How do you know when you're getting angry?

HASSAN 5.23:   When, you know, when somebody goes on and on and on about something and that really gets me pissed off.

RICK 5.24:   Okay. Okay. So when people start pushing you and pushing you and pushing you.

HASSAN 5.24:   Right

RICK 5.25:   Probably you can take it once or twice.

HASSAN 5.25:   Right. But after that, I probably want to take off their head or something.

RICK 5.26:   Yeah. Yeah. And I think we need a backup plan for you after she pushes you two to three times. To say, "Hey, we need to take a time out."

HASSAN 5.26:	Alright.
RICK 5.27:	I mean, you need to take a time out. So how does that sound?
HASSAN 5.27:	Yeah, but, take a time out when I'm talking on the phone, or . . . hang up on her or what?
RICK 5.28:	Well, I don't know if hanging up on her will be a good idea. But I am wondering if you need to say, "Hey, I'm getting angry right now and I don't want to be angry. Can I hang up and call you back in ten minutes?"
HASSAN 5.28:	Yeah. It sounds reasonable. I guess.
RICK 5.29:	So . . . what do you mean, "it sounds reasonable".
HASSAN 5.29:	I can try to do that but I don't know if I'll . . .(laughing) I mean, when I get angry I get in, you know, in the heat of it.
RICK 5.30:	Well, you may not do it perfect, and that's okay. But if you know that you have this strategy, my guess is that when you start getting angry you're gonna remember it sometime. And then you can say, regardless of when it happens - if it's right at the beginning, or you're right in the middle of being angry - saying, "Wait a second. We're not getting any place right now. I don't want to be angry with you because I need to see my kids. Can we hang up or can we stop this for right now and come back in ten minutes and talk about it."

The goal of this segment is to increase Hassan's sense of control; control rests on his belief that he can be successful. Rick works to ensure Hassan's success by using small steps to build the plan and continually checking to assess Hassan's ability to carry out the plan. The practice on what he intends to say to his former wife allows Hassan to gain confidence and increases the chances he will be successful. As the segment closes, Rick attempts to relieve Hassan's anxiety by helping him understand that he does not have to be perfect. This support is important to help stabilize Hassan's weak but growing sense of control.

Step 6: Obtaining Commitment

This segment centers on carrying out the plan that has been developed. Rick asks Hassan to repeat the plan to check that he knows the plan. In order to increase the chances of the plan's success, they discuss a specific time and method to talk with Hassan's former wife. This process allows potential problems to be identified and to prevent these from happening. Finally, Rick returns to the issue of Hassan using drugs again and strongly encourages him to attend a meeting and contact his sponsor. Hassan is open to those recommendations and makes plans to attend a meeting that afternoon and call his sponsor.

Observe the way Rick supports and encourages Hassan during this segment. Rick knows Hassan's confidence is very fragile and wants to ensure as much as possible that he is successful. Note the change in Hassan's mood when the session ends, as his problem solving skills begin working again.

RICK 6.1:   So now, what are you going to do? (pause) We've talked about a lot of stuff.

HASSAN 6.1:   Tell her, I won't be angry (laughing) . . . when I'm angry, I just need to take, you know, hey, when I am angry we're not getting anywhere. So, I'll call you back later or something.

RICK 6.2:   Okay, yeah, well, we actually talked about four things so far, okay?

HASSAN 6.2:   Okay, okay, alright.

RICK 6.3:   We talked about how your gonna approach her in the first place. Let's do this engineering, step-by-step.

HASSAN 6.3:   Okay.

RICK 6.4:   "This is . . . you know I understand you're angry right now, I understand I haven't been paying the kids. I have disappointed you, and I've disappointed myself. But, I need to see the kids because I need their support right now cuz this is really tough for me."

HASSAN 6.4:   Okay. Seeing. Doing that part when I first call her.

RICK 6.5:   Right. Right.

HASSAN 6.5:   Okay. Okay.

RICK 6.6:   And then you're gonna have to give her, feed her some facts.

HASSAN 6.6:   Okay, I've been looking for jobs, I got resumes out there. Do the workshop things. Um, constantly looking, you know, trying to find a job.

RICK 6.7:   Yeah. "And you, you just need to be patient with me." Um, I'm wondering if you need to say something . . . and I don't know, about this, if you're gonna. . . willing . . my guess is you'll have to but . . . willing to make up the child support.

HASSAN 6.7:   Yeah, I'm gonna have to. That's not a problem, I just need some to pay it.

RICK 6.8:   Okay.

HASSAN 6.8:   No problem paying it.

RICK 6.9:   Okay.

HASSAN 6.9:   You know.

RICK 6.10:   And that you're not blowing smoke, you mean this.

HASSAN 6.10:	Right. "I mean it. I'm not, you know. . . I'm sincere. I'm not blowing smoke and I just want to be able to see my kids."
RICK 6.11:	Okay. So, you . . .
HASSAN 6.11:	". . . see our kids."
RICK 6.12:	Yeah, yeah. Well, yeah, well, that might be a better way to do it. Even to say "our kids" rather than "my kids". Um, so you're gonna tell her you understand, give her some facts. What's the backup plan if she gets angry?
HASSAN 6.12:	I'm gonna tell her, um, "You know, I know I haven't, you know, been doing everything I ought to do and I know that it's been difficult for you but, you know, please just be patient with me. You know, I'd like to try to, you know, see my kids, see our kids, and make this, make this work."
RICK 6.13:	Okay. Okay, what are you going to do if you're angry?
HASSAN 6.13:	I'm gonna, um, take some time . . . time out for myself, I guess. Yeah. Tell her, "Hey, I just need some time, I think . . .I'm getting angry. You know, it's not being productive right now, so I'll call you back later."
RICK 6.14:	Okay, okay. So, now, when are, when, when do you think you can do that?
HASSAN 6.14:	Well, I can do that, probably, later today, I guess.
RICK 6.15:	Later today?
HASSAN 6.15:	Yeah.
RICK 6.16:	What time? This afternoon sometime?
HASSAN 6.16:	She won't be home, I guess . . .I won't call her at work, I guess . . . in the evening.
RICK 6.17:	Okay, probably wouldn't be a good idea to call her at work. That's not a good idea. So, call her this evening.
HASSAN 6.17:	Um hum.
RICK 6.18:	What time does she get home?
HASSAN 6.18:	She gets home about six or so after she picks up the kids and everything. So, you know, probably later on in the evening around eight or something like that.
RICK 6.19:	Okay, they'll be finished with dinner and everything?
HASSAN 6.19:	Yeah.
RICK 6.20:	You won't be interrupting.

HASSAN 6.20:	Right.
RICK 6.21:	Okay. Will the kids be in bed . . . they'll be up . . . you know.
HASSAN 6.21:	They'll be up, probably doing their work or watching TV or something.
RICK 6.22:	Okay, okay. So probably around between eight, eight thirty, or so you can call her. So you get yourself ready to do that.
HASSAN 6.22:	Um hum.
RICK 6.23:	Okay. You know, Hassan, there's one other thing that I think might be important for her. You know, and the reason you came in today. Cuz you were afraid of using.
HASSAN 6.23:	Right.
RICK 6.23:	I'm wondering if maybe you need to tell her your plan that you, if you can figure out a plan that you have in place so that you're not gonna use.
HASSAN 6.23:	That I'm not gonna use?
RICK 6.24:	Yeah.
HASSAN 6.24:	(pause) I guess, plan would be, I guess, you know, to go ahead to work the program, I mean.
RICK 6.25:	Work the program?
HASSAN 6.25:	Yeah. Yeah.
RICK 6.26:	Yeah, but I imagine you've said that to her before.
HASSAN 6.26:	Yeah.
RICK 6.27:	You have to give her some concrete stuff. You came in and see me today. You came into the place where you got treatment before because you were afraid and you needed some support.
HASSAN 6.27:	Yeah. I can do that.
RICK 6.28:	Maybe tell her about that. . . talking with me.
HASSAN 6.28:	Yeah. Can you sign something for me? Or, uh, get a little note that I was in today?
RICK 6.29:	I think I can do that.
HASSAN 6.29:	Okay. That would be helpful.
RICK 6.30:	We can, we can write something that, "Hassan came in, we talked." I'm wondering if maybe tomorrow, we need to set up another time for you to

come in. Just to kind of follow-up on what's going on. See how the plan worked. See if we need to re-engineer it or anything.

HASSAN 6.30: Okay, that's fine. I think I would need that.

RICK 6.31: Okay.

HASSAN 6.31: Cuz, I'm, you know, that close.

RICK 6.32: Yeah, I know, I hear you're that close. But, you know you've done hard things before.

HASSAN 6.32: Right.

RICK 6.33: You've stayed clean four years. And I imagine there have been tough times in those four years.

HASSAN 6.33: Right, very tough times.

RICK 6.33: Yeah, and you've been able to get through it.

HASSAN 6.34: Yeah.

RICK 6.34: This is just another tough time you can get through. You don't need to think anything a week, two months from now. You just need to think the next 24 hours.

HASSAN 6.34: Okay.

RICK 6.35: Work the program that way. Day by day.

HASSAN 6.35: Yeah.

RICK 6.36: What about a meeting? Going . . . you know of any meetings today?

HASSAN 6.36: Yeah, there's a meeting later this afternoon. At the church here.

RICK 6.37: You think you can get to that?

HASSAN 6.37: Yeah, I can get to that.

RICK 6.38: Okay, okay. Anything else you can think of?

HASSAN 6.38: Hmm (pause) I don't know, maybe I can call my sponsor. I haven't talked to them, to my sponsor in a while.

RICK 6.39: That's a good idea. Good problem solving. Okay. Anything else that we need to talk about, or?

HASSAN 6.39: No, I think, I think it's been helpful.

RICK 6.40: And then I'll see you here tomorrow morning.

HASSAN 6.40:   Okay.

RICK 6.41:   Okay? And think Ed may be in tomorrow morning too, so maybe the three
                    of us can meet together.

HASSAN 6.41:   Okay.

RICK 6.42:   Okay? Does it sound like a good idea?

HASSAN 6.42: Sounds good. Thank you.

Although fragile, Hassan's confidence and feelings of control have significantly increased. The
defeatist attitude he began with has shifted to one of hopefulness and expectancy. A follow-up
session with Hassan's previous therapist and Rick is set for the next morning. This session will enable
Rick to check on the success of the plan as well as shore up and continue to stabilize Hassan's
confidence.

Reflection Questions

1. *Describe the similarities and differences in these two case scenarios.*

2. *Compare the approaches used by the crisis workers in these case scenarios. What similarities and differences
   can you identify?*

3. *What would you do different if you were the* crisis worker in both scenarios?

APPENDIX A

Core Listening Skills

Core Listening Skills

Core listening skills are used to facilitative listening and responding to client comments in each of the six steps. The skills we find most useful in crisis intervention are restatement, reflection of feelings, owning statements, summary recapitulation, open-ended/close ended questions, and monitoring non-verbal clues. Individually and combined these skill enable us to elicit as much information from clients as possible about their current state of coping. These basic counseling techniques are critical in establishing a bond of trust between the often emotionally out-of-control, confused client and the crisis worker. For some of you the following description of these skills will be a review, whereas for others this may be the first time you have been introduced to core responding skills. Yet, the importance of these skills cannot be overemphasized. Being knowledgeable and proficient in these skills are critical for effective crisis intervention.

a. Restatement.

Restatement takes the client's own thoughts and words about the content of the event and feeds them back to the client from the crisis worker. This technique is important in letting clients know they are understood and also allows the crisis worker to determine what he or she heard is indeed correct from the client's perspective.

> CL: Nobody seems to understand or care what happens to me. It's like I've been shunned by everybody that ever cared for me just because I made one mistake and got hooked on crack.
> CW: Right now you feel isolated, even outcast by all the significant people in your life. They can't forgive you for using drugs.

b. Reflection.

Reflection of feelings seeks to understand and uncover client feelings. Most often phrased in the form of a guess or a hypothesis, reflections are set in a conditional sense so the client is free to except or reject the proposed feeling state hypothesized by the crisis worker. While this is a core facilitative technique in standard exploratory counseling and is commonly used in crisis intervention with people who are having trouble expressing emotions, it may be counterproductive for clients in crisis who are already emotionally charged and ventilating. In that regard, with clients who are emotionally out-of-control, further amplification of emotionally charged material is probably best avoided. Note the difference in the client's response in the following two examples.

In the first example, the client is attempting to make a decision about attempting to reestablish a relationship with his parents. By touching on the feelings of embarrassment and shame, the crisis worker opens some extremely hurtful long held feelings and behaviors to awareness and discussion.

> CL: I just don't know if I can go back and talk to my folks. After what I've done. Stealing from them. Lying . . .
> CW: It sounds like it would be tremendously embarrassing to meet them face to face. It's almost as if you're too ashamed to try to make amends.
> CL: (Starts to weep). I don't know. I can't forgive myself for what I did to them how in the world could they forgive me for all the hurt and pain I have caused.

In example two, the client is extremely agitated. The crisis worker's response does nothing but pour emotional kerosene on an already blazing emotional fire.

94

CL: How could she turn me into the cops! Send me to jail! To jail, by God! My own mother.
CW: You feel she somehow betrayed you.
CL: (Pounding his fist on the table and rising up out of his chair) Well, what the hell would you think if it was you dumb cluck? That no good uncaring traitorous bitch. No wonder I started using dope.

Notice how the crisis worker's response takes the focus away from the client and focuses instead on the mother. Responding to the client that keeps the focus on him might be more effective.

CL: How could she turn me into the cops! Send me to jail! To jail, by God! My own mother.
CW: That really surprised and hurt you.
CL: You can say that again. I thought she was suppose to love me. I must be a real loser if my own mother can't love me.

c. Owning statements.

Owning statements are typically "I" statements that indicate the crisis worker's state of being in regard to what is happening in real time. Owning statements are used much more in crisis intervention than other therapy forms because the crisis worker often has to take control of the situation and make clear declarative statements about what is occurring or what needs to occur. Owning statements may indicate the crisis worker's current state of understanding.

CW: Right now I'm puzzled. You say your medication is making you sick, but you are unwilling to go to the hospital to get it changed.

Owning statements may also be used to reinforce behavioral compliance.

CW: I really appreciate it that you put the pipe wrench down, Jake. I believe you have the courage to really resolve this problem peaceably.

Owning statements may also be used to set behavioral limits and maintain personal integrity.

CW: You asked for help, but when you continuously yell, swear, and refuse to calm down, I wonder if we should go on with the session until you have more control.

Owning statements are often assertion statements that ask for compliance when the client is too out of control to effectively govern his or her behavior.

CW: Brandishing that pipe wrench is really getting in the way of me helping you out. I need for you to put the pipe wrench down now!

Owning statements may also be value judgments. While in a perfect, stable counseling setting, the crisis worker would refrain from making value judgments, in the world of crisis intervention, the crisis worker often makes value judgments about client's when their emotions, behaviors, and thinking are faulty and are further aiding the crisis.

CW: If what I hear you saying is correct, that will get you a go-to-jail card for a long time. I don't believe that would be in your best interests and I don't think you believe so either when you really think about it.

d. Summary recapitulation.

Summary recapitulation attempts to summarize the content of the client's current affective, behavioral, and cognitive functioning. It encapsulates what the client has, is, or will feel, do, or think about the problem. It clarifies for both the client and the crisis worker what the current state of events is that surrounds the crisis. Either the crisis worker or the client, if able, may do the summary.

> *CW:* So overall what is happening right now is that you're pretty depressed because this is your third attempt at rehab and kicking the crack habit. You want to quit desperately and keep telling yourself that but then you can picture and feel the rush you get and finally give in and fall off the wagon, particularly when you get depressed thinking about your family and friends giving up on you. Right now the future seems hopeless.

e. Open ended and closed questions.

Open ended questions are used to gather information regarding clients' affective, behavioral, and cognitive reactions to the crisis. These responses may also be in the form of a statement requesting clients to say something more about their reactions. Closed questions are used when crisis workers need specific information.

> *CW:* What would you like to see for yourself in the future?

A closed question is:

> *CW:* How long is it until you usually relapse?

f. Minimal encouragers.

Minimal encouragers are used to communicate to clients that you are attending to them. Generally very short, one or two words, these responses convey support as clients tell their story. Often times these minimal encouragers can be used when clients pause to help them continue their story.

> *CL:* I am not sure what to believe any more. Everything is going to hell. Nothing is going right my wife won't let me see the kids and...
> *CW:* Go on.
> *CL:* I really love my kids. I know I don't say that but I do. I wish I would have been able to say that when I got to see them all the time...
> *CW:* Okay.
> *CL:* I am really dumb. Why couldn't I have seen that sooner.

g. Monitoring nonverbal cues.

Use of basic exploration techniques may be daunting since many crisis clients are not very receptive to verbal interaction with the crisis worker. In that regard, a great deal of patience and ability to monitor subtle nonverbal cues is often necessary.

> *CW:* While you haven't said anything, I can't help but notice the way you are wringing your hands and the grimace on your face indicate there is some real heavy duty thinking go on. We have plenty of time. I know it is difficult to talk about, but I want you to know I will wait as long as need be for you to tell me what has happened.

To use nonverbal cues while doing crisis intervention on the telephone crisis workers must rely on their hearing and follow-up questions rather than vision. Listening for background noises such as pacing may indicate a client is angry or anxious. The confirmation of the interpretation of the footsteps can be done by reflecting a feeling or asking a question.

> *CW:* You seem to be pacing. I wonder if you are feeling angry about something?

Voice quality such as tone, speed, and pitch are also ways to use nonverbal behavior when working with clients on the phone. Again, the lack of visual substantiation requires crisis workers to verify their interpretation through questioning clients.

> *CW:* As fast as you are talking right now makes me think you are anxious. How does that fit for you?

APPENDIX B

Triage Assessment Form: Individuals

TRIAGE ASSESSMENT FORM: CRISIS INTERVENTION
©R. A. Myer, R. C. Williams, A. J. Ottens, & A. E. Schmidt

CRISIS EVENT:
Identify and describe briefly the crisis situation: _____
_____
_____

AFFECTIVE DOMAIN
Identify and describe briefly the affect that is present. (If more than one affect is experienced, rate with #1 being primary, #2 secondary, #3 tertiary.)

ANGER/HOSTILITY: _____
_____
_____

ANXIETY/FEAR: _____
_____
_____

SADNESS/MELANCHOLY: _____
_____
_____

Affective Severity Scale

Circle the number that most closely corresponds with client's reaction to crisis.

1	2	3	4	5	6	7	8	9	10
No Impairment	Minimal Impairment		Low Impairment		Moderate Impairment		Marked Impairment		Severe Impairment
Stable mood with normal variation of affect appropriate to daily functioning.	Affect appropriate to situation. Brief periods during which negative mood is experienced slightly more intensely than situation warrants. Emotions are substantially under client control.		Affect appropriate to situation but increasingly longer periods during which negative mood is experienced slightly more intensely than situation warrants. Client perceives emotions as being substantially under control.		Affect may be incongruent with situation. Extended periods of intense negative moods. Mood is experienced noticeably more intensely than situation warrants. Liability of affect may be present. Effort required to control emotions.		Negative affect experienced at markedly higher level than situation warrants. Affects may be obviously incongruent with situation. Mood swings, if occurring, are pronounced. Onset of negative moods is perceived by client as not being under volitional control.		Decompensation or depersonalization evident.

BEHAVIORAL DOMAIN

Identify and describe briefly which behavior is currently being used. (If more than one behavior is utilized, rate with #1 being primary, #2 secondary, #3 tertiary.)

APPROACH: _____
_____
_____

AVOIDANCE: _____
_____
_____

IMMOBILITY: _____
_____
_____

Behavioral Severity Scale

Circle the number that most closely corresponds with client's reaction to crisis.

1	2	3	4	5	6	7	8	9	10
No Impairment	Minimal Impairment		Low Impairment		Moderate Impairment		Marked Impairment		Severe Impairment
Coping behavior appropriate to crisis event. Client performs those tasks necessary for daily functioning.	Occasional utilization of ineffective coping behaviors. Client performs those tasks necessary for daily functioning, but does so with noticeable effort.		Occasional utilization of ineffective coping behaviors. Client neglects some tasks necessary for daily functioning is noticeably compromised.		Client displays coping behaviors that may be ineffective and maladaptive. Ability to perform tasks necessary for daily functioning is noticeably compromised.		Client displays coping behaviors that are likely to exacerbate crisis situation. Ability to perform tasks necessary for daily functioning is markedly absent.		Behavior is erratic, unpredictable. Client's behaviors are harmful to self and/or others.

COGNITIVE DOMAIN

Identify if a transgression, threat, or loss has occurred in the following areas and describe briefly. (If more than one cognitive response occurs, rate with #1 being primary, #2 secondary, #3 tertiary.)

PHYSICAL (food, water, safety, shelter, etc.):
TRANSGRESSION ___   THREAT ___   LOSS _____

_____
_____
_____

PSYCHOLOGICAL (self-concept, emotional well being, identity, etc.):
TRANSGRESSION ___   THREAT ___   LOSS _____

_____
_____
_____

SOCIAL RELATIONSHIPS (family, friends, co-workers, etc.):
TRANSGRESSION ___   THREAT ___   LOSS _____

_____
_____
_____

MORAL/SPIRITUAL (personal integrity, values, belief system, etc.):
TRANSGRESSION ___   THREAT ___   LOSS _____

_____
_____
_____

Cognitive Severity Scale

Circle the number that most closely corresponds with client's reaction to crisis.

1	2	3	4	5	6	7	8	9	10
No Impairment	Minimal Impairment		Low Impairment		Moderate Impairment		Marked Impairment		Severe Impairment
Concentration intact. Client displays normal problem-solving and decision-making abilities. Client's perception and interpretation of crisis event match with reality of situation.	Client's thoughts may drift to crisis event but focus of thoughts is under volitional control. Problem-solving and decision-making abilities minimally affected. Client's perception and interpretation of crisis event substantially match with reality of situation.		Occasional disturbance of concentration. Client perceives diminished control over thoughts of crisis event. Client experiences recurrent difficulties with problem-solving and decision-making abilities. Client's perception and interpretation of crisis event may differ in some respects with reality of situation.		Frequent disturbance of concentration. Intrusive thoughts of crisis event with limited control. Problem-solving and decision-making abilities adversely affected by obsessiveness, self-doubt, and confusion. Client's perception and interpretation of crisis event may differ noticeably with reality of situation.		Client plagued by intrusiveness of thoughts regarding crisis event. The appropriateness of client's problem-solving and decision-making abilities likely adversely affected by obsessiveness, self-doubt, and confusion. Client's perception and interpretation of crisis event may differ substantially with reality of situation.		Gross inability to concentrate on anything except crisis event. Client so afflicted by obsessiveness, self-doubt, and confusion that problem solving and decision-making abilities have "shut down." Client's perception and interpretation of crisis event may differ so substantially from reality of situation as to constitute threat to client's welfare.

101

DOMAIN SEVERITY SCALE SUMMARY

Affective _____   Cognitive _____   Behavioral _____   Total _____